IRELAND'S HEARTBEAT

2015

Published by WORD of the LORD WinePress
IRELAND
Webpage: www.thewordofthelord.biz
Email: wordofthelordwp@gmail.com

©Copyright of individual poems, songs and all other forms of writing and art belongs to author indicated on each page.
Pen, music note, St. Patrick and shofar illustrations © by JONATHAN MULLEN
Child in the womb © (p 32) by BERNICE HEAPHY
Diamond illustration © (p 120) by LYDIA MCDOWELL

© Copyright of collective work, 'Ireland's Heartbeat 2015' belongs to WORD of the LORD WinePress publisher.

Scripture quotations:

NIV – Holy Bible, New International Version®, NIV® Copyright © 1973, 1978, 1984, 2011 by Biblica, Inc.® Used by permission. All rights reserved worldwide.

NLT – Holy Bible, New Living Translation, copyright ©1996, 2004, 2007, 2013 Used by permission of Tyndale House Publishers, Inc., Carol Stream, Illinois 60188. All rights reserved.

NKJV – New King James Version Copyright © 1982 by ThomasNelson, Inc. Used by permission. All rights reserved.

NRSVBCE – New Revised Standard Version Bible: Catholic Edition, copyright © 1989, 1993 the Division of Christian Education of the National Council of the Churches of Christ in the United States of America. Used by permission. All rights reserved.

ESV – The Holy Bible, English Standard Version Copyright © 2001 by Crossway Bibles, a publishing ministry of Good News Publishers.

AMP – Amplified Bible Copyright © 1954, 1958, 1962, 1964, 1965, 1987 by The Lockman Foundation. Used by permission (www.Lockman.org)

We, the publishers, aim to produce books that will build up the body of Christ, encouraging a fresh infilling of the Holy Spirit, hearts revived in the love of Jesus and lives restored to Kingdom principles. We do not necessarily agree with every view expressed by the authors or with every interpretation of scripture made, but expects each reader to make his/her judgement in the light of their own understanding of God's love and in an attitude of Christian love and fellowship.

ISBN: 978-0-9575494-3-2
Cover design © by LYDIA MCDOWELL
Printed in the UK

To friends, and friends of friends,
Throughout this, our Emerald Isle,
And far beyond . . .

LOVE is taking the blame
Even when it's not yours to carry

HOPE is believing God's resolve
Will not be long to tarry

JOY is laughter of the soul
Even in the midst of mire

PEACE is the power placed deep within
Enabling you to walk through the fire

Thanks . . .

Firstly, THANKS to the WRITERS who contributed to this anthology. Without you, this project would have been impossible! I love the depth of spirit with which so many of you write.

Thanks to LYDIA MCDOWELl who was able to design the front cover based on the picture in my head - very well done! (It's very beautiful.)
    The meaning behind the front cover design is that whilst Ireland is physically small, it is made great when acting under the anointing of Heaven, affecting the whole world for good. God has very good plans for our island and when we allow our heartbeat to be in tune with His, we will be very blessed indeed.

Thanks to the artists who submitted artwork alongside their writings and greater thanks to those who provided artwork for others.

Thanks to JONATHAN MULLEN for designing the stamp size symbols for the pages (they're beautiful):-
    Quill pen for poetry and story
    Music note for songs
    St. Patrick for writings associated with St. Patrick
    Jewish shofar for prophetic writings

Thanks to PETRA HAKE who prepared the music sheets for printing and RÓISÍN JENKINSON who prepared all the portrait photos and illustrations. You both did a wonderful job.

Thanks to RUTH CHIPPERFIELD and ANNA BRUNNOCK who helped with proofreading.

And last, but not least, THANKS TO MY WONDERFUL PAPA, for giving me this exciting project, to pass a little bit of my time upon the earth.

Contents

Acknowledgements 4
Introduction 13

PART 1 THE VOICE OF THE PEOPLE

Rosemary Alcorn
    Stand Before Your Gaze 17
Festus Alohan
    Have your way 18
    Fill this place 19
    Turn to Jesus 20
Meaghan Ballangher
    Giant 21
Birinder
    Jacob da khhoh/Woman at the Well 24
    hare hare khet/Green Pastures 25
Joan Bradley
    An Irish Question 26
    The Tourist 27
    The Grey Stone Wall 28
Paschal Coffey
    In Memory of Imelda 29
    The Peacemakers 30
Teresa Dillon
    'Questions and Answers' 31
    Justice for the wee, unborn baby 32
Trevor Durejaye
    Because of You 33
Ayobola BE Elegbede
    God of Creation 34
    One Heart 36
    An African Night Affair 38
    Igba Ope/An Offering of Thanks 39
    Praise Him 42

Tunde Esho
    Freedom   44
    I'm Amazed   45
John Faris
    The English Cemetery at Rajkot   46
    Ovoca Manor   47
Ailish Farrelly
    Run   48
    An Rud is Annamh is Iontach . . .   49
Carol Farrelly
    Dance Caged Souls Dance   50
    No Human   51
Dorothy Forsuh
    Move On Up   53
    In the Bosom of Your Heart   55
Mary Gavin
    Game of Life   56
    God's Landscape   57
    Holy Spirit   58
    Life on the Dole   59
    The Baton of Faith   61
Tomasz Grzymkowski
    Proza Życia   62
    Prose of Life   63
Mike Harper
    Jesus   64
    Holy Land   65
Bernice Heaphy
    He Dwells There   66
    Dear Jesus   67
Louis Hemming
    Cillini   68
Leslie Howard
    Threshing Floor   69
    Lift up the name of Jesus   70
    Through the crowd   71
    You alone are God   72
    Melt this heart   73
Shirley Howitt
    I'll Soar like an Eagle   74

Christine Ikwunwa
    Ngcwele,Ngcwele/Holy,Holy   75
Róisín Jenkinson
    Bound   76
    Journey   77
    Red   78
    Vivid   80
Amanda Clarke
    The Holy Shoe   81
    Jesus with Me   82
Carrie Kelly
    The Fountain of Life   83
    The Robot Society   84
    Words   85
    The Forest of Life   86
    The Old Man   87
Wilma Kenny
    The Father's Love   88
    God Among us   89
    The Master's Seal   90
    Strawberry Clove   91
    Healing Touch   92
Dermot Landy
    Here is my Heart   93
Vincent Lyons
    Heart Surgery   94
    Framed   95
    Intertwined   96
Thos Maher
    The Grey Heron   98
Cailin Ní Thallúin
    Say 'No!' to 'Gay-Marriage'   99
    Water, Water, Everywhere   100
Brendan Marrett
    The Ghost of the Unsaid   101
    When all this is over   105
    Oh, yes please   105
    Interpretations   107
    The Scarecrow, a sonnet   108
Lynne Mary-Lou
    Eyes to See   109

Nobby	110
Taking All the Credit	112
How He makes my heart delight	114
Anne McCracken	
Saying Goodbye	116
The Awakening	117
Suzannah McCracken	
Shine on Bright Spirit	118
Rebellion	119
The Uncreated Arrives	120
Awakening the Slumbering Bride	121
I dreamed a dream	122
Geraldine McDaid	
Caring Hands	124
Home	124
John McDaid	
Why?	125
Lydia McDowell	
Who Is He?	126
You are Mine	127
Emma McGlynn	
Tom	128
Harland & Wolff	129
The Final Launch	130
Rosaleen McGuinness	
Dark Night of the Soul	132
Connemara Healing	133
Do Not Be Afraid	134
Holding Back	135
Rainbow	136
Brian Millar	
Please Speak to Me	137
In Realms Beyond	138
And He Shall Reign	139
To My Wife	140
Ruth Millar	
True Beauty	141
Worship	142
Jonathan Mullen	
The Call	143

June Murphy
- Because of the Lord's great Love — 144
- As the Deer — 146
- Named — 148

Rebecca Oluwaseyi
- Lift Him Higher — 149

Ines Bouhannani
- Sonderangebot: Alles Zum Halben Preis — 150
- Special Offer – Buy One Get One Free — 151

Seán Ó Ceallaigh
- Sweet Season with us Stay — 152
- September Sadness — 153
- Christmas Day! — 154
- The Christmas Crib – Revisited — 156

Stephen O'Brien
- From God to the Children — 158

Damien O'Neill
- True Treasure — 159

Gerard O'Shea
- At Last . . . The Sea — 160
- An April Day — 161
- Market Forces — 162
- Mother — 164

Mary Oyediran
- The Widow in our midst! — 165

Len Pearson
- Wonderful love — 168
- Think Green — 169
- I'm Not Sorry — 170
- Embers — 171
- O, Tribune of Rome — 172

Shay Phelan
- Sparrows — 173
- The Treasure in the Earthen Vessel — 174
- Lord of Agape — 175
- The Sword that Slays the Enemy — 176
- More Beautiful the face of Jesus — 178

Sarah-Jayne Pomeroy
- The Land of Milk and Honey — 179
- Goodbye Belfast — 181

Kenny Rasaki
- Bless You Lord   183
- Jesus, halloweth be your name   184

Mark Davy
- Jesus   185

John Purcell
- The Robin   186

Philip Robinson
- Still Faith is   187
- Reasonable News   188
- Father You are Sight   189

PJ and Pauline Sexton
- Teach Me to Love   190
- At His Throne   191
- The Day of Victory Is Coming   192
- Eternity   193
- The Potter and the Clay   194
- Just As   195
- Time for Jesus   196
- Number Nine   197
- Love Is the Answer (song)   198
- Cords of Human Kindness   199

Roger Skillington
- Generosity toward God   200
- Adoration   201
- Our God Is   202
- Christian Rap   203

Harry Smith
- He walks the land . . .   204
- Listen!   205

Brenda Vanwinkle
- The Sound, the Scent of Green   207
- Turning   208
- Open   210
- Glee!   213

Brendan Creed
- A Different View   214
- Song for Breakthrough in Your Life   215
- Are You Going to the Wedding Feast of the Lamb?   217
- Bring in a Harvest   219

    The Way   220
Petra Hake
    God's Love   221
    With All   223
    Why?   225
Merry Bradley
    If You Want a Happy Song   227
    Prayer to Holy Spirit   229
    Draw Close   231
Princess Lewa
    Thank God, I'm Free!   232
R. Seathrún Mac Éin
    Is Iontach Grás ('Amazing Grace' in Irish)   234
    Will You Dare to Follow Jesus?   235
Margaret Boles
    At the Bus Stop   236
    Wet Evening on the Ha'penny Bridge   237
    I Want to Be Young Again!   237
    No Parking   238
    Blossoms on the Bin   239
    Important People   240
Ruth Chipperfield
    Gordon, Business as Usual   241
Robert Creed
    The Train   246
    Pain   248
    Sleeping   250
    Amazing   252
    The Sound of Ireland   253

PART 2 THE VOICE OF THE YOUNG
'A Day in the Life of a School Kid' Competition: 256
Holly Mae Chippendale   257
Ivy Joy Hake   258
Sofia Maher   259
Emma Duffy   260
Joshua Bradley   262
Laura Farrelly   263
Samuel McNabb   264
Méabh Ní Scathghail   266

Jona F Hake	267
Lynda Collins	268
Year 9 students, Ashfield School	269
Karis Hake	270
Virginia O'Connor	272
Melinda Huian (short story)	273
PART 3 THE VOICE OF THE LORD	275
Introduction	277
St. Patrick's Confession	278
Saints Patrick and Bridget	280
Paul Kyle	
O Ireland	281
1700s-1800s	282
Twentieth Century Words	283
Brenda Vanwinkle	
A Song of Ireland	284
Twentieth Century Words (continued)	287
Roger Skillington	
A Word for Cork	291
Twenty-first Century Words	292
Lynne Mary-Lou	
God Speaks	295
Olivia Ralph	
Moments	296
Twenty-first Century Words (continued)	297
Anonymous	
Blessings	306
Twenty-first Century Words (continued)	308
Sarah O'Neill	
What are You Doing Here, Elijah?	309
Twenty-first Century Words (continued)	311
Prophecies for 2015	313
'St. Patrick's Breastplate' (English)	316
'St. Patrick's Breastplate' (Irish)	317
'Christ with Me' in 6 languages	318
End notes	319
Bibliography	320

Introduction

What a privileged person I am to compile this anthology! Last summer it was nothing more than an off-the-cuff suggestion, in response to an email from Amanda Clarke seeking advice on publishing a solitary poem the Lord had given to her. Other than the usual route of magazines and newspapers, I wasn't able to give any new direction. I added, almost as an afterthought, that I knew a few poets in the land. Maybe, in the future, they could group together to create a book – when in the future, I had no idea. Little did I know that in making the suggestion, the seed was sown, ready to blossom this spring.

Annually, I spend time with my Lord and Master, Jesus, His Father and precious Holy Spirit, to see what He would like me to do in the year ahead. My major priority for the early part of 2015, God ordained, was to compile this anthology of spiritual songs and poems, named 'Ireland's Heartbeat 2015', and then take it on a tour of Ireland mid-year, showcasing the great talent God has given to the land and people of Ireland. Christians, from all different church backgrounds and cultures, living in Ireland would be invited to submit poetry and song, alongside Irish immigrants and their distant cousins in foreign lands, as well as ministers to and lovers of our Emerald Isle. In recognising the multi-cultural society we live in, Gaeilge, Ireland's ancient tongue, would be recorded alongside newer languages spoken across our land (all with English translation, of course). In the hope that this collection would give greater insight into Christianity in Ireland than the decennial census undertaken, children and young people would also need to be represented. As a springboard for their creative input, I set a competition, 'a day in the life of a school kid', for children and youths of school-age to enter. School need not necessarily be mentioned. The intention was to encourage young people to share life through their eyes, so basically any subject was acceptable. This again was set for children living in Ireland and those living abroad who have Irish blood in them. Aspiring writers responded, some voiced youthful concerns, while others simply shared the highs and lows of a kid's day.

When I began collecting people's works in January I thought, maybe, thirty people would submit songs and poems. I am still amazed that almost three times that number responded! First time writers rub shoulders with award-winning poets. Together they form a beautiful rainbow of literary colour. Alongside accolades to God, and appreciation of nature, are family and society issues–the joys of life and pain of death, miscarriage and abortion, bullying, and the modern-day slavery of human trafficking. In representing current affairs of 2015 in particular, poems are also included recording society's reaction to the new water charges, as well as giving a Christian response to the 'Gay marriage' referendum to be held in May 2015.

I asked one anointed worship leader if she had written any songs. 'No', she replied, 'but I have many prophecies that have come forth in worship. You can use them, if you want.' I knew immediately that her suggestion was part of God's plan.

At first I thought prophetic words, knowledge that comes by way of supernatural revelation from God, rather that the product of mere human intelligence, learning or experience, would be dotted throughout the book, but soon realised it should have its own section. Therefore three sections have developed:

The Voice of the People (adult songs, poetry and biography extracts)
The Voice of the Young (young people's songs, poetry and one story)
The Voice of the Lord (God's voice over Ireland, from Patrick to today)

Just as prayer is intended to be a two-way conversation, it makes perfect sense to me that after humans share their thoughts and feelings, we should allow God to share His heart for our land and people. Prophecy can be about the past, present or future. St. Patrick heard God's voice directing him for himself and for the lives of the people of Ireland, in his own lifetime and beyond. Nothing has changed–God still speaks. (One poem I have chosen to be displayed in the 3rd section is actually entitled, 'God speaks'.) I've brought together the ancient writings of Patrick with the modern-day prophecies of native Irish and visiting ministers, to encourage Ireland in the truth that God has a plan– a very good plan, for our nation. Lastly, I include St. Patrick's Breastplate in different languages, representing once again people from many different nations that have made Ireland their home. This multi-cultural society in which we live could not have been envisioned even twenty years ago. For us to get the very best out of our situation, we must actively embrace our diversity and appreciate the differing qualities each group brings, especially in the family of God.

I hope you enjoy this wonderful collection of writings.

Katey Moreland
WORD of the LORD WinePress publisher
April 2015

The Voice of the People

I said to the Lord: "You are my God;
Hear the voice of my supplications, O Lord . . ."
                              Psalm 140: 6 NKJV

Ireland's Heartbeat 2015

Key to symbols on each page:

Songs

Poems/creative writing

St. Patrick's writings
and St. Patrick's Breastplate

Prophetic writings

ROSEMARY ALCORN

STAND BEFORE YOUR GAZE

Lord, You are Majesty and Mercy,
You bought me, broken, filthy.
In Your Presence, I will rise.

Chorus: Now help me stand, help me stand before Your gaze,
So You can heal me.

Lord You've won this heart of mine,
Conquered by Your love divine.
Now take me —all of me.

And help me stand, help me stand before Your gaze.
I'll let You love me.

Oh to know You more like this!
Your Word, it is Your Kiss.
Mature me in Your love.

And let me gaze on You, let me gaze on You!
Till love is all I am.

Isaiah 33: 17

ROSEMARY ALCORN, LIMAVADY, NORTHERN IRELAND

57 years young, retired from working as a physiotherapist, Rosemary now cares full-time for her mother. When working, she took time out to do mission training and outreaches, with church, OM, and YWAM and also spent time at the International House of Prayer. The Lord gave Rosemary the verse above while she meditated on God's desire, and her need, to fully look on Him without fear or shame, since He gave Himself to completely cleanse and heal and set her free.

Festus Alohan

Fill this Place

Fill this place
 With your presence Lord
It's Your presence that we need
Fill this place with your presence Lord
It's Your presence that we need
Fill this place
Fill this place
Fill this place with your presence
Fill this place
Fill this place
Fill this place with your presence

> *And the priests could not enter the house of the Lord, because the glory of the Lord had filled the Lord's house.*
>
> *2 chronicles 7: 2NKJV*

FESTUS ALOHAN

HAVE YOUR WAY

Have your way oh Lord
Have your way
Have your way oh Lord
Have your way

You are the Potter
We are the clay
Mould us and make us
After your will

Have your way, oh Lord
Have your way
Have your way, oh Lord
Have your way

You are the Potter
We are the clay
Mould us and make us
After your will

Father, have your way
Jesus, have your way
Holy Spirit, have your way
Have your way, oh Lord
Have your way
(Repeat)

"Look, as the clay is in the potter's hand, so are you in My hand, O house of Israel!

Jeremiah 18: 6NKJV

FESTUS ALOHAN

Turn to Jesus

Turn to Jesus and be saved
Oh oh oh Ireland
Turn to Jesus and be saved
Oh oh oh Ireland
He is God and there is no other
He is God and there is no other
So turn to Jesus and be saved, Ireland

*"Look to Me, and be saved,
All you ends of the earth!
For I am God, and there is no other".*

Isaiah 45:22

FESTUS ALOHAN, DROGHEDA, IRELAND
Born into a pagan family in Nigeria, Festus had a supernatural encounter with the Lord Jesus at the age of 29, gave his life to Jesus and started a journey of intimacy and faith with him. He was a Bible school director for many years in Egypt until God ask him and his wife, Amy, in 2009, to move to Ireland, taking up full-time intercession to prepare the way of the Lord for the revival that He want to birth forth in Ireland. They arrived with one child, Josiah, but the Lord blessed them in Ireland with 3 more children, Joy, Jonathan and Jeremiah.

MEAGHAN BALLANGHER

GIANT

Hard surfaces of hexagonal rock lay beneath my feet,
they surround me,
fanning out,
fading down,
a pure promising picture of God's endless creativity.

Behind me rise the great green guardians,
magnificent and mysterious they loom,
protective yet perilous,
beautiful yet fractured.

They are a witness to,
wonder,
preoccupation,
frustration,
impatience,
longing.

I am not the only one who notices,
breathes,
absorbs the unexplainable magic of the rocky
hills,
the spraying sea,
the stacked stones, so perfectly placed.

There are others;
a man and a woman,
an arm around a waist,
eyes crinkled,

feet planted upon the highest peak;
a girl, solitary,
hands placed outward,
camera in fist,
tiny in stature,
awe imprinted upon lovely eyes.

Sea foam sprays casting a glimmer,
a peek into the perfect,
unpredictable future,
the brilliant sun bursts,
beams
streams of untainted
crystal rays.
A fine drizzle
floats bewitchingly,
glinting like shattered bits of glass.

I stand there,
lightly drenched,
alone,
with thoughts of Him,
that master craftsman.

I have no pad of paper,
no pencil,
nothing but myself.

I can't help but look around,
I have new eyes,
pure, clear eyes.

I see Him everywhere now,
in a baby's rosy cheeks,
in a lover's lips,
in a broken swing,
in a mother aging,
in a disaster,
in a pain-filled family.

He is everywhere.
How could I not see this then?

> --Inspired by the Giant's Causeway

MEAGHAN BALLANGHER, ONTARIO, CANADA

Meaghan is a young poet and writer. Her poetry is a natural expression of her faith, heart, and love. Her recent month-long mission trip to Northern Ireland inspired her poem "Giant's Causeway". Eternally blessed by a land of vivid greens and generous and hospitable people, Meaghan counts Northern Ireland and its people as a home away from home. She is currently taking a gap-year after finishing high school and is planning on, with God's blessing, attending university for social work in the fall.

BIRINDER

JACOB DA KHHOH/WOMAN AT THE WELL

IN PUNJABI:
Mein Jandi si khhooh te bharan paani
din raat raundi si meri jaan ajanni
ki milya menu khhoh te de kol
ki milya menu sarovaraan de kol
yeesu milya menu boliaa do bol te ditta sub kujh,
menu miliya subh kujh
kiuon jande ho khhoh te, kiuon jande o sarowaran wul
aao mere yeesu kol uthe milega sub kujh
aao mere yeesu kol uthe hi heh subh kujh
aao ohda paani pio milda hai muphtt, ham muphtt
te tehan mitt jangian, han, tehaan mitt jangian jindgi bhar dian

IN ENGLISH:
I used to go get water from the wells
Day and night my soul used to cry
What did I get from those wells?
What did I get from the holy wells?
Jesus met me, HE spoke two words:
 'Just believe' and 'Give me everything'

I've received everything now (complete)
Why do you go to the well, why do you go to holy wells?
Come to my Jesus; you will get everything
Come to my Jesus; HE has everything for you
Come.... drink water from HIM , its free, yes its free
You wouldn't be thirsty again, ever again

> *. . the water that I shall give him will become in him a fountain of water springing up into everlasting life.'*
>
> *John 4: 13*

HARE HARE KHET/GREEN PASTURES

IN PUNJABI:
yeh hare hare khet, yeh neela aasman
Labhdi haan mere piyar da cherah din raat
dine yeh saare rung rolenan ich
raatin saundi haan pur dil jagda, oode piaar wich din raat
 jidaan oh swaragan wich te men haan ithe dunia wich
door door ik dooje ton pur naal naal hur pul
swarag vi swarg nahin je othe yeesu nahin
mein vi mein nahin, je mein mere yeesu di nahin

IN ENGLISH:
In these green fields and beautiful sky
I am seeking my lovers face.
In such a hustle and bustle during the day,
At night I sleep, but my heart stays awake in HIS love.
As HE is in heaven, I am in this world -
So far away from each other, yet we are together every moment.
Heaven wouldn't be heaven if Jesus was not in it.
It's a waste of my being if I am not of my Jesus.

> *I sleep, but my heart is awake;*
> *It is the voice of my beloved! . . .*
>
> Song of Songs 5: 2

BIRINDER, CO. LEITRIM, IRELAND

Born in India in a traditional Sikh home, Birinder's life dramatically changed at 17 when her father died and her mother committed suicide. In the midst of these tragedies, she was taken to England. An Irish woman of faith introduced Birinder to the God of Miracles. Birinder was called to Ireland in 2008 and is grateful to be called to be an intercessor and loves to worship He who is Love, in dance. She has 4 beautiful children.
Contact her at b3mine@hotmail.co.uk

JOAN BRADLEY

An Irish Question

What is buried in this heart of mine
that struggles for my place of birth?
Some planetary pull, my stary sign
imprinting codes of heavy worth?

History full of things long gone to rest
upon the soil of this small isle,
imbueing it with dread, passion dressed,
to surface now in surges wild.

Inheritance, an island filled with strife,
blood stained soil cried out for more,
draining Celtic children dry of life.
What is burning in my core?

Is it earthy soil, or power I crave,
kill and maim by fellow man?
Is it sentiment, arising brave,
to flames my feelings like a fan?

If I could probe the deepest depth and find;
bring to light its vital source,
find this damaged gene of human kind,
isolate this primal force.

Imprint it deep with peace and active power
to stop this hurt of man and earth.
Conceive a seed immune to crass desire,
so future children come to birth.

Only 'The Creator' knows the code
to rectify this strife within,
hate, that hungers in my heart for blood.
In seeking Him will Ireland win?

Psalm 46:9

JOAN BRADLEY

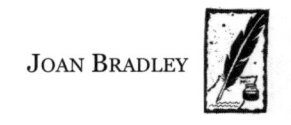

THE TOURIST

Had they come from - USA?
Returned exiles? As they may!
Camera swinging, map in hand,
Tinted clothing, pale and grand.

Peering around as if to see
a wonderful sight. Obviously
he limped, she gently leaned
upon his strength it seemed.

What had they done to reach this day?
Toiled with hope that come what may
they would return, seek out their home.
Or satisfy desires to roam.

What had it cost to fill this view?
Their youthful strength, used up too
their vigour, now they'd reached the end.
Was it worth the body rend?

The spend of life what does it mean?
Seeing all the world is certain gain.
To reach one's roots, of value too.
Is that the end for me, for you?

Without a hope that when its done
another form will rise and run
in life upon a higher plane,
earthly aim has little gain.

> 'And what does the Lord require of you? To act justly and to love mercy and to walk humbly with your God.'
>
> *Micah 6:8*

THE GREY STONE WALL

A weight of stillness seeped into heart and mind.
Sunday morning in early summer, going to church.
Noise and stress of everyday was stilled.
Behind drawn curtains people slept.
A calm had come that could be felt.
The early sun easing the aches of life.
  The clack of shoes the only sound,
Except for 'the click'.
  The click of a tricycle as she rocked it
Back and forward,
Back and forward, a few inched from a wall.
  She was intent, gazing into the stonework.
  An old wall built with grey stones.
  Our eyes met in silence then:-
  'Have you seen MY stone?' she asked.
  Stooping down I saw it,
A piece of quartz sparkling in the sun.
  It spoke of happy things, diamonds, stars, joy in God.
  I had not found it, never would, I was too tall.
Her stone, a gem, in a grey stone wall.
  'It's beautiful', I said.
  I went on my way,
Our brief encounter over, she cycled away.
  The clack of my shoes,
And the click of her tricycle blending,
Our lives enriched.

Psalm 8:2

JOAN BRADLEY, DUBLIN, IRELAND

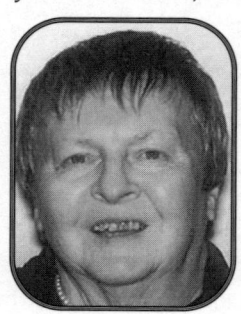

"I am a senior citizen living in the centre of Dublin city. I accepted Jesus Christ into my life as a teenager and it changed my life. The Lord has been my strength, helper and friend ever since. I do not know how I would have coped with life's challenges without Him. I have been engaged in Christian writing for some years. I also help with the Irish Christian Writers' Fellowship; to encourage Christian Writers, particularly those writing in Ireland for Ireland."

PASCHAL COFFEY

IN MEMORY OF IMELDA

Imelda is taken from us to her true and eternal home.
She is mourned by friends and family and by those who have no home.
Her death is to us an amputation without an anaesthetic,
but letting go eventually brings healing that is thorough.

Her family supported her with love true and unfailing,
helped her become the person, who showed others their greatness.
Her possessions here were modest, but she still enriched us all.
The gift of loving friendship is a pearl that cannot be bought.

Suffering made Imelda better rather than bitter.
When life closed certain doors God opened many others.
Imelda entered new doors with joy and great thanksgiving,
through the portals of death to new creation living.

She crossed her own desert to the promised land of compassion,
an enlightening journey to rapport and understanding.
Both close friends and strangers and strangers felt at home with Imelda.
She fed the lonely and hungry with her warmth and her empathy.

True love is not blind, but really super-sighted.
Imelda saw greatness in people others thought blighted.
Her loving acceptance helped them see their true worth.
In Imelda's sweet presence one always felt good.

She has left us fond memories 'till we meet her in heaven.
We release her to God and to Jesus, Our Saviour.
We yield to rhythms unforced of both nature and grace
and receive from God's Spirit true healing and peace.

2 Cor 1: 3-4

Imelda was a good friend of mine, a very cheerful and friendly person, who had to leave her job because of a physical disability. She retained her serene and pleasant disposition despite all inconveniences and both friend and stranger felt at home in her company. She died at a comparatively young age.

PASCHAL COFFEY

THE PEACEMAKERS

Blessed are the Peacemakers.
They are everybody's friends but nobody's fools
Their meekness is not weakness
but power and strength under true control.

Yet they bring not peace but deep division.
They divide us from the enemy within us.
Their pure light exposes our dark rash judging,
Our labels and prejudices take a pounding.

They destroy our mindsets, yet love us as people.
They are radical revolutionaries, yet truly gentle.
They absorb our venom, but take no offence,
As they mirror back our ugliness.

They stir hornets' nests that may sting to death.
But peacemakers reign even in death.
Their pure goodness will always reproach us.
We can banish them from the earth but not from our conscience.

But not even these can compare with The Prince of Peace,
The self-sacrificing scapegoat for all evil deeds.
Like a poultice He draws our guilt and our sin,
Through loving forgiveness that gives true peace within.

~inspired by Martin Luther King
Matthew 5: 44-45

PASCHAL COFFEY, CORK, IRELAND

Paschal is a retired secondary school teacher. He studied for the priesthood for five years in Maynooth, where he received the unearned gift of an intimate, personal relationship with Jesus. He taught religion and Irish mainly. He has also written over 20 playlets based on Gospel scenes, which have been acted out in the classroom and in churches. He hopes to publish these in the near future.

Teresa Dillon

Questions and Answers (Poem to John Bowman)

I've watched your programme many a night
And always felt you did alright
By letting every point of view
Be aired while helped along by you.

A good presenter is, I know,
A person who can run the show,
And give all sides an even chance
To say their piece and take a stance.

With questions on abortion theme
I may be wrong, but it does seem,
With you plus three guests on the show
The odds are always for the pro.

I think you should have two and two,
While you withhold your personal view.
Yes, pin-point things from every side,
Then leave the people to decide.

What Europe think, I'm not concerned,
By their mistakes I hope we've learned,
Abortion hasn't cured their ills,
Their next step - - - euthanasia pills!

The media, alias God, all know,
Just say we're backward, dense and slow,
You have a very powerful voice,
But we the people have the choice.

Don't call us stupid 'cause we care,
The right to life is only fair.
To hell with all the media fuss,
I hope we pick what's best for us.

Justice for the Wee, Unborn Baby

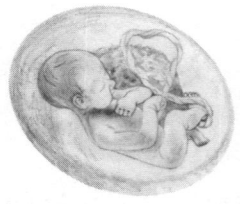

With no judge or jury, no trial or appeal
For the wee unborn baby—no justice, I feel
Pro-abortion and pro-choice, they're all out in force
Helped by most media outlets, of course
As if fifty million dead isn't enough
We need to be modern and take all their guff
They talk of free speech in the great public square
Except for the churches or people who care
We're regarded as heartless, divisive and dumb
'cause we want all the babies alive when they come
Mothers are told that it's their 'Right to choose'
Pop over to London—you've nothing to lose
But the silent majority need to stand strong
'cause to terminate babies just has to be wrong
Now some of these girls are alone and in shock
So don't vilify all—have pity—don't knock
Politicians will change like the weather, we know
As most have no guts—they will go with the flow
Sure our country and values have gone—now we find
That all the foundations have been undermined
Wake up and be counted before it's too late
Try and stop the decline—and close the flood gate

Psalm 139: 13

TERESA DILLON, Co. KILKENNY, IRELAND

Teresa Dillon, a widow with two grown up children, currently runs the family farm near Freshford, Co. Kilkenny and writes poetry in her spare time. Teresa wrote her poem 'Questions and Answers' after feeling distressed and helpless in watching how one-sided a TV debate was on the abortion referendum back in 1992. Sadly, over two decades later, this fairness cannot be found for children within the womb and so Teresa follows her first poem with one entitled, 'Justice for the wee unborn baby'.

BECAUSE OF YOU

When it was dark all around
There was no one to help me
You showed up and showed me love
In my mind I thought there was no point in living
But You wrapped Your hands around me and showed me love

Chorus: see I found my way around because of You
You're the only one who showed me love
When nobody else would
I found my way around because of You, it's because of You
Because of You

Everyone else thought I was good for nothing
But you showed Yourself strong in my life You did me right
The world was against me You took the fight
I owe you my life my heart my soul
Take it

Chorus / Bridge: found my way x12 / Chorus...

TREVOR DUROJAYE, DUBLIN, IRELAND

Trevor is a 23 year old musician whose love for music has grown with him. Originally from Nigeria, Trevor likes to think Ireland raised him and so considers himself Nigerian-Irish. The eldest of four children, he writes his own songs as well as for other artists. Trevor has recently released a single titled 'Awesome God', appreciating God in his life and for saving him from a terrible car crass in April 2014. Follow Trevor and his musical journey on
IG : waleg24 Facebook: Trevor Durojaye
FB like page: Trevorsmusic

AYOBOLA 'BE' ELEGBEDE

GOD OF CREATION

1. Trees in the field bowing down to You
Beasts in the wild lifting eyes to You
Fishes in the seas swimming unto You
Birds in the sky lifting up Your name
Singing out Your praise
Whiter than snow, purer than gold
Older than time, sweeter than wine
Lord that's who You are
And You always are

Chorus 1
Every nation
Bow in adoration
Every generation
Exalt the God of creation
Because He's worthy
To receive glory

2. Mountains so high exceeding measure
Valleys so deep filled with great treasure
Water so clear covering the earth
Creatures great and small daily giving birth
Cause You give them breath (yes You give them breath)
Stronger than love, reaching from above
Faithful than friends even till the end
Lord You never change
You remain the same

Chorus 2
Young and old
Stand be bold
Tell of His love
You He did mold
Let His praise flow
For His greatness shows

Bridge
Lord I look to heaven and I see
The angels and elders bow to You
Lord I look to the sky and I see
Sun and moon and all stars adore You
Lord I look to the land and I see
Every man, woman and child praising You
Singing You are the God of creation
The God of creation

Rap
He is the God of all creation
Clap your hands to the only one creator
The heavens You dwell in
Your blessings unending
The earth's Your footstool
You're the reason I pull through
From Oshodi to Ebute Meta
I pass 3rd Mainland Brigde
I no fall inside water
What else can I say
Na You be my Oga
And You is my Father
I call You my Teacher
So I say let every living thing
With every breath you breathe
Gather from far and near
Whether you slim or fat
Either you tall or short
(Yeah) Don't matter what you are
You need to give Him your all
He is your creator

Chorus 3
Every nation bow in adoration
Young and old stand be bold
Every generation tell of His love
Because He's worthy
To receive glory
Let His praise flow
For his greatness shows
He's the God of creation
The God of creation

Psalm 145: 4

Ayobola 'BE' Elegbede

One Heart

1. Emi ba l'egberun ahon
Ko to fun iyin Re
Emi ba l'egberun owo
Ko to gb'oruko Re ga
Emi ba l'egberun ese
Ko ma to royin Re o
Sugbon hun o yin O
Pelu okan mi

Chorus (English translation of above):
If I had a thousand tongues
That ain't enough to praise Your name
If I had a thousand hands
That ain't enough to raise Your name
If I had a thousand feet
Ain't enough to spread Your news
But with this one heart
I will worship You

2. If I were ten thousand stars
That ain't enough to shine Your light
If I were ten thousand men
That ain't enough to show Your might
If I were ten thousand years
Ain't enough to search Your ways
But with this one heart
I'll serve You all my days

3. Though I had a load of sin
That couldn't stop Your grace
Though I had a hateful soul
That couldn't stop Your love

Though I have a matchless power
You still rule from up above
So with this one heart
I will love You more

Bridge
A thousand tongues, a thousand hands
Ain't enough to praise
Ten thousand stars, thousand men
Couldn't show Your might
A load of sin, a hateful soul
Wouldn't stop Your love
But with this one heart
I will worship You

B'emi ba l'egberun ahon
Ko ma to fun iyin Re
B'emi ba l'egberun owo
Ko ma to gb'oruko Re ga
B'emi ba l'egberun ese
Ko to royin Re
Sugbon hun o yin O
Prlu okan mi

(Repeat Chorus)

But with this one heart
I will worship You
(till fade out)

Psalm 99: 2-3

Ayobola 'BE' Elegbede

AN AFRICAN NIGHT AFFAIR

The night is dark
The sky is black
The moon so bright
As it sheds its light
In the quiet of the shadow
The crickets chirp and bellow
All animals drawn in midnight trance
Coming each with its mate to dance

I awake to the music
I arise to its lyric
Where oh where is my love
Where oh where is Adebayo*
That we may drink of the fountain of joy
That we may eat of the bread of pleasure
That we may speak of love with action
And share its fruits with passion

Come my husband and lover
Come my friend and brother
Come before the night is turned to day
Come before the dark is gone away
Before we must again wait
And again say
The night is dark
The sky is black

*Nigerian name pronounced a-dey-ba-yor

Song of Solomon 3: 1-5

AYOBOLA 'BE' ELEGBEDE

IGBA OPE (Yoruba language, Nigeria)	AN OFFERING OF THANKS (English translation)
(Solo) Mo gbe'gba ope tan E, Baba Mo gbe'gba ore tan E o Mo gbe'gba ope Mo gbe'gba iyin Mo gbegba ore tan E o *Chorus* Mo gbe'gba ope tan E, Baba Mo gbe'gba ore tan E o Mo gbe'gba ope Emi gbe'gba iyin Mo gbe'gba ore tan E o *(Choir 2ce)* 1. Emi dupe o *(3ce)* Mo dupe Baba Emi dupe o *(3ce)* Mo dupe o *(Solo 2ce)* 2. Temi tope o *(3ce)* Mo dupe Baba Temi tope o *(3ce)* Mo dupe o *(Choir 2ce)* 3. Oro mi ju ope lo *(3ce)* Mo dupe Baba Oro mi ju ope lo *(3ce)* Mo dupe o *(Choir 2ce)*	*(Solo)* I bring You an offering of thanks, Father I bring You an offering of gifts, oh Father I bring an offering of thanks I bring an offering of praise I bring an offering of gifts, oh to You *Chorus* I bring You an offering of thanks, Father I bring You an offering of gifts, oh Father I bring an offering of thanks I bring an offering of praise I bring an offering of gifts, oh to You *(Choir 2ce)* 1. Oh, I am grateful *(3ce)* I'm grateful Father Oh, I am grateful *(3ce)* Oh, I'm grateful *(Solo 2ce)* 2. Oh, I should be grateful *(3ce)* I should be grateful Father Oh, I should be grateful *(3ce)* Oh, I am grateful *(Choir 2ce)* 3. I am more than grateful *(3ce)* I am more than grateful Father I am more than grateful *(3ce)* Oh, I am grateful *(Choir 2ce)*

Yoruba:	English:
Oh, oh, oh....oh *(Solo)*	Oh, oh, oh....oh *(Solo)*
Chorus (Choir 1ce)	*Chorus (Choir 1ce)*
Bridge Hun o yin O *(3ce)* Emi, hun o yin O *(Choir 2ce)*	*Bridge* I will praise You (3ce) I, I will praise *(Choir 2ce)*
Mo yin O *(2ce)* Baba Mo yin O, mo yin O *(Choir 3ce)*	I praise You (2ce) Father I praise You, I praise You *(Choir 3ce)*
(Solo) Lord I praise You Lord I praise You Lord I worship Lord I praise You Lord I lift You high Lord I praise Your name Lord I bless You Lord I praise You Lord I thank You	*(Solo)* Lord I praise You Lord I praise You Lord I worship Lord I praise You Lord I lift You high Lord I praise Your name Lord I bless You Lord I praise You Lord I thank You
Oh, oh, oh....oh	Oh, oh, oh....oh
Chorus (Choir 1ce)	*Chorus (Choir 1ce)*

(Solo)
Mo gbe'gba ope.....eeee
  (Choir [same time])
   Mo gbe'gba ope
	(Solo)
	I bring an offering of thanks
	  (Choir [same time])
	   I bring an offering of thanks

(Solo)
Yeah, yeah.......yeah
  (Choir [same time])
   Emi gbe'gba iyin
   Mo gbe'gba ore tan E o
	(Solo)
	Yeah, yeah.......yeah
	  (Choir [same time])
	   I bring an offering of praise
	   I bring an offering of gifts

IGBA OPE/AN OFFERING OF THANKS

(continues in English . . .)

Hallelujah (3ce)   Hallulujah *(echo 3ce)*
We praise You   We praise You
Hallelujah (3ce)   Hallelujah *(echo 3ce)*
Lord we thank You   We thank You

Hallelujah   Hallelujah
I love You   Hallelujah
I bless You   Hallelujah
I adore You   We praise You
I bow before You   Hallelujah
I glorify You   Hallelujah
I thank You   Hallelujah
Lord I sing   We thank You

I worship
I worship You Lord
You mean all to me
There's none like You
You're the lover of my soul
The keeper of my heart
Lord I worship You
Lord I bless You

Therefore by Him (Jesus), let us continually offer the sacrifice of praise to God, that is, the fruit of our lips, giving thanks to His name.
Hebrews 13: 15

All of Ayobola's songs can be found on her album, Igba Ope, released in 2012

Ayobola 'BE' Elegbede

Praise Him

E dide, ka yin Baba lo go...o
(Solo)

1. From the rising of the sun
Until its going down
From the east unto the west
Let His holy name be blessed
He's high above the heavens
He shines above the stars
I'm gonna lift His name up high
(Solo 2ce)

Chorus
Praise Him
Come on and praise Him
Come on and praise His holy name
Come on and praise Him
Come on and praise Him
Come on and praise His holy name

2. Your steadfastness oh God
Extends above the earth
Your faithfulness my Lord
Goes beyond all known breath
You're King and You're Master
You reign now and ever
I'm gonna lift Your holy name up high

Chorus (Choir 2ce)

Bridge
La, la, la....la
(Solo)

Praise Him with the lyre and the harp
Praise Him with a shout and a clap
Praise Him when you're sad and you're glad
Come on and praise the Lord
Praise Him with the flute and the string
Praise Him with a song that you sing
Praise Him for He's God and He's King
Let everything that has breath in it praise the Lord

Chorus (Choir 2ce)

Praise Him, praise Him, praise His holy name
(Until fade out)

Psalm 150

AYOBOLA "BE" ELEGBEDE, CO. CAVAN. IRELAND
Ayobola first encountered gospel music as a teenager, while attending secondary school in Nigeria. In 1996, Ayobola moved to Germany and joined the Lighthouse Fellowship choir in Mulheim, Germany. There, the Holy Spirit began to teach her to hear and write inspirational songs and poems. Ayobola's songs in this anthology are from her album, 'Igba Ope' (An Offering of Thanks) released in Dublin, Ireland, in August, 2012. Ayobola is happily married, blessed with lovely children and continues to be inspired by the Holy Spirit.

TUNDE ESHO

FREEDOM

Look at me
Spreading my wings
Learning to fly I am free
Just look at me I belong to a king
I can testify, I am free
The beauty of freedom x4

Yes I'm free at last, thank my master, thank my pastor
No more playing around, no joker I am not a clown
Back in father's house, Christian, no longer sired to klaus
My Jesus broke the hold now I run from sin Usain Bolts
I'm free, he's free, she's free, we all free
Shout it out from the roof

Look at me
Spreading my wings
Learning to fly I am free
Just look at me I belong to a king
I can testify, I am free
The beauty of freedom x4

Like water I am free
Like Mandela I am free
Oga at the top he came for me
Calmed the sea and made me see
It's not over till he says it's over
Could be in bondage and drive a land rover
So now I'm checking myself
Go ahead, check yourself
I got my freedom now it's your turn to come and get it

Look at me spreading my wings
Learning to fly I am free
Just look at me I belong to a king
I can testify, I am free

The beauty of freedom x4

I'm Amazed

Take my hands use them as you please
Cuz I've seen what you can do when I believe
I was lost all the way down to the ground
It was you that gave me my full release
Now I'm free to say I have my liberty
No weapons formed against me, shall prosper
And I'll never be the same again
He's taken away my shame
God do your thing
Don't wanna stop the flow
You're capable of anything
My life's in your hands
And I wanna show the world
You're so beautiful
You turned my life around
Words cannot explain how I feel ~ I'm amazed

It is for freedom that Christ has set us free . . .
Galatians 5: 1

Tunde Esho, Dublin, Ireland

Born January 1991, Tunde has always had a passion for music and life. Brought up in church, he lived a double-life as a teenager - a Christian at home, a gangsta with his friends. During that time he was part of a rap group. In 2008, at a crusade with his church in Dublin, he rededicated his life to Christ. His music followed. To date he has released two mixtapes, one EP and one album. As well as been an artist he is also a producer and studio engineer. God is only starting with him.

'Freedom' and 'I'm Amazed' come from Tunde's album, 'There to Here' released in 2014, the excellent feedback of which prompted a nationwide tour.

JOHN FARIS

THE ENGLISH CEMETERY AT RAJKOT.

Grass grows among the graves
At the English Cemetery at Rajkot.
Irish visitors bring garlands and posies,
Gifts of welcome and respect from Indian friends
To lay on the graves
Of missionaries and children
In the cemetery at Rajkot.

It is explained
That a baby was born on 16th March
Who only lived some weeks
And emotion overflows
That I share a birth date
With my great grand aunt.

Another grave nearby
For a boy aged one year and two days
And moving around I see
His parents lost another child
Who lived for two months
And I weep to write of that.

And we who are parents wonder
Could we like Abraham offer up Isaac
And the younger people are very quiet.

We pray, we sing, we look and walk away
With one last look back
At the grass and fading flowers
On Irish graves in the English cemetery at Rajkot.

The grass withers, the flower falls
But the word of our God always lasts

And I will trust in you always.

Ecclesiastes 3: 2

JOHN FARIS

OVOCA MANOR

This is a special place.
Above the road and railway
We hear their sounds
But leave them as background noise
To scents of trees and grasses
Symphony of green and light.
Children call and sometimes cry.
There is pain in falling even here,
But this is a place
For binding wounds and easing pain.
My friends are here
And my special friend.

> John writes: "As a family we enjoyed many summer 'Family Weeks' at Ovoca Manor organised by Scripture Union. Among the activities there were poetry workshops, out of which came the poem *Ovoca Manor*. The reference in the last line is to Graham Kendrick's *I'm special* which we sang there. I hope people can work out who the *'special friend'* is."

"*The English Cemetery at Rajkot* was written after a mission trip to Gujarat, India. My great-great-grandparents (James & Mary Glasgow) were one of the first Irish Presbyterian missionary couples to Gujarat, and buried their first two children there. The reference in the last line is to Stuart Townend's *The Lord's my shepherd*, a song we sang in the graveyard. It is touching to see how deeply the Indian Christians value those who travelled so far and sometimes suffered much to bring them the good news of Jesus."

JOHN FARIS, CORK, IRELAND

John Faris was born in Belfast in 1952, studied in England and Scotland and was Presbyterian minister in Co Fermanagh before moving to Cork in 1988. He is married to Heather and they have two children, Naomi who teaches English as a foreign language in Cork and Peter who works with OfCom in London.

AILISH FARRELLY

Run

Get Ready!

There was Light,
night and day
BEFORE the sun..

Yet battles are waged,
though the war has been won.

The leaves are turning so quickly now,
I've never heard them make so much noise!

The oil on your heads
the black blood of the Earth
is burning!

-RUN!-

How unfamiliar the rain felt last night
Like floodgates after a drought..
Like the first rains!!

HAVE NO DOUBT

The Master is returning
to His house!!!

If My people who are called by my name will humble themselves and pray and seek My face, and turn from their wicked ways, then I will hear from heaven and will forgive their sins, and heal their land.

2 Chronicles 7:14

An Rud Is Annamh Is Iontach
(What is Rare is Wonderful)

Slowly sailing . . .
 drifting by the shore
 . . . le do thoil.
(if you please)

Breezy thinking . . .
surfing waves so old
 . . . is fearr cairde ná ór.
(friends are better than gold)

In search of all truth . . .
or what lies to be found
 . . . ar m'anam.
(upon my soul)

Out in some soggy Sunday oaisis . . .
tháinig mo ghrása le mo thoabh!
(my love came to my side!)

 I woke unto a dream,
ar muir is ar tír . . .
(on land or on sea)

Maireann croí eadrom i bhfad!
(the light heart lives long!)

Proverbs 3:6

Ailish Farrelly, Co. Leitrim, Ireland
Ailish lives a quiet and simple life in County Leitrim with daughter Laura and all their pets! She came to that life changing place of redemption and salvation in autumn 2008 at the age of 26. Since then life has been about remembering how blessed we all are and trying to keep everything in perspective as she waits in worship for the return of our Messiah Yeshua. She says, "He's coming SOON! All glory to Father God, Yeshua his son the Messiah and Ruach ha-Kodesh his Holy Spirit, my best friends."

CAROL FARRELLY

THE DANCE IN ME

© Masha Duna

Dance caged souls, to the true meaning of life
Dance across the hot coals, to the other side of strife
Dance tip toed giving God your heavy bearing load
Move in a different way to the motions of everyday
Linger in the movement, holding each moment to its end
Feel what it is to feel, dance what it is to dance
Let go, let the spirit flow, in the veins of your beating pains
Warming your heart from the bitter cold
Seek and regain the pureness that life has stained
The fluency of joy, regret can't obtain
Dance and rejoice, how awesome you have a choice
Listen to your souls sound, what an amazing grace
Do not be ruled by fear, it is not your leader
Use your ears to hear, and your eyes to see
That, that cannot be heard and that, that cannot be seen,
Is God's dance for you, believe in your dream
Dance it, it is of thee in you
Feel free to breath, now there is more need
For your fruit growing tree to plant more seeds
I hope you can see in this short glance
That this is your chance
Dance caged souls Dance!

Psalm 149: 3

CAROL FARRELLY

No Human

Tulips colouring the blind
Nature's music soothing the unhearing
Birds dancing in the air with the wounded
Water falling with laughter
Numbness being reawakened
Love in hands being there to hold
Long enough to heal 7 fold
Everything is going to be ok

Shadows are no longer dark
Willows no longer weeping
What is, is and what isn't, isn't
No more in-between or hiding
Inside beauty is surviving
Being revealed like a siren

Come and go within and listen
Quiet your mind and just listen
Underneath all the noise
Beyond all the reasoning
Away from all wanting
Closed off from all distractions
And listen just listen
What do you hear?

We know we know we know
There is more
Something above all we see
And something above all that again
It's there within all along
A constant inner song
Giving you meaning
A reason to never feel unloved or empty again

Because no Human can fulfil this
No human can tell you yours
No human can do what God does
So choose to listen and not ignore
Explore that inner gift of meaning
Fulfilling, comfort and protection
Only you can hear yours
So take responsibility and listen
Just listen

Psalm 139: 2

CAROL FARRELLY, CO. LEITRIM, IRELAND
Carol was born in the States, but grew up mostly in the beautiful, peaceful, countryside of lovely Leitrim. Carol has always enjoyed being creative in life and co-creating with the Creator. She sees creativity and dance as a form of prayer and way to connect with God. She feels blessed for the gift of faith and this wonderful opportunity to share two of her poems about such topics with others. 'Dia Daoibh' - (God be with you all!) :-)

DOROTHY FORSUH

MOVE ON UP

Part I
(Lead & Choir)   Stacatto/Sharp/Crisp and drumming without symbals

Chorus   Movin' x4   echo   Movin' x4   echo
Move-Movin'! Movin'!' Movin'! Movin'!   echo
Move-Movin'! Movin'!' Movin'! Movin'!   echo
Movin' x4   echo

MOVE! ON! UP!   Choir
To hear his voice and then obey and . . . Lead   (Response choir)
MOVE! ON! UP!
To Testify and Glorify, you. . . Lead   (Response choir)
MOVE! ON! UP!
With Offering, Tithe and Seed Giving to . . . Lead
Working and giving and sharing our lives unto God . . . (Lead & Choir)
Chorus   Movin' x4   Movin' x4   Movin' x4

MOVE! ON! UP!
Spirit-filled man from mortal body. . .   MOVE! ON! UP!
With courage, strength you stand your guard and . . . MOVE! ON! UP!
And Character good without corruption . . .
. . . Perse-verance, Long-Suf-fer-ing, Kindness and Love; All for God.
Chorus   Movin' x4   Movin' x4   Movin' x4

MOVE! ON! UP!
With Holiness you cannot fail but . . .   MOVE! ON! UP!
With hearts awake for understanding . . .   MOVE! ON! UP!
You run the race to get the prize and . . .
....Death swallowed up and our victory is unto the Lord . . .!
I said, Death swallowed up and our victory is unto the Lord . . .!

Part II (Rap)
If you wanna move on up you let the blind lead the blind;
leave the carnal of the Christian-discern a wolf in sheep's' clothin'
Whoa!!! Here come the Pharisees and Sadducees Y'all . . .
Get ready for Canaan Land - Egypt is dead in the water.
   The Rock has come to save and set y'all free.
   . . . . I said death is swallowed up - our victory is unto the Lord.

Part III
Choir - intense MF   You gotta move on up
You gotta push on up
You gotta give something up   x3
You gotta . . . (loud) MOVE IT!

Part IV (Rapper & Choir)
Movin' x4 . . .   soft/intense....continuous (under)

Rap Calls Out (over)
My heart is clean. I got my deliverance.
Be separate from the wicked yah-all.
Man, I is just talkin' parables.
Talk up Jesus y'all. Herodias there ain't no deal! . . . (end of under)

BECAUSE THIS SEED CAN-NOT FAIL! . . . . . . (drumming) . . . . . .
IT –IS- FINISHED!!   (All or Rapper only)
(If solo rapper, choir holler/whoop at the very end)

2 Peter 1:3-8

The song '*Move on up'* was divinely inspired by the Holy Spirit. Its contemporary gospel style appeals to the younger Christian generation. The song reveals how a believer can resist the wiles of the enemy and grow more in the Lord.

Dorothy Forsuh

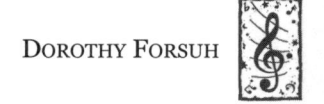

In the Bosom of Your Heart

In the fullness of your love
I have Joy
In the place that I have Peace
there is rest.
and when you hold me close to you
All my cares are far away.
In the bosom of your heart
Keep me Lord.

'Yes, I have loved you with an everlasting love;
Therefore, with lovingkindness I have drawn you;'
Jeremiah 31:3b

Dorothy Forsuh
Co. Galway, Ireland

Dorothy is an ordained minister of the gospel and worship leader. She and her husband Joseph are both involved in church planting. They are based in Connemara in the west of Ireland. She is passionate about the message of souls not missing heaven.

Mary Gavin

Game of Life

We're there for each other
in times of need
to put others first
and do a good deed.

Like the ebb,
and the flow of the tide
we must give and take,
talk and confide.

Soft spoken words
and a shoulder to lean on
may be what you need
when you feel put-upon.

The one in your family
who's the thorn in your side
makes you look at yourself
and not go and hide.

Someone pushes our buttons
which are there to be pressed,
inviting someone to come
and to be our guest.

Like the rocks in the ocean,
causing the waves to tumble,
we're all shook up
and complain and grumble.

But without the odd shake,
we face stagnation.
The silt builds up
and hinders progression.

Spiritual Songs, Poems and Prophecies

Looks like we're all
part of a plan
helping each other
be better woman or man.

Like pawns on a chessboard
our future depends
on who's around us
before the games ends.

God's the guy
who's playing the game
our spirits comply,
our wills to tame.

'... iron sharpens iron ...'

Proverbs 27: 17

'I wrote this after realizing how much we, as human beings, need each other. Often when we get annoyed at a comment somebody makes it can open our mind to a broader view and make us look objectively at ourselves.'

GOD'S LANDSCAPE

Soft subtle fresh greens
Spring forth
while the cool blue of the sky
is blended on the mountainous horizon.

Reds, pinks, oranges and lilacs,
Summer colour vibrancy.
Glowing sunsets burst forth
energizing sea and sky.

Shades of gold and brown
evolve from the autumn palette.
Watercolours in the rain
are dried by the gusty winds.

Highlighted snow capped mountains
brushing deep blue winter skies.
contrast with the shadowy landscape
on the earthly canvas.

Isaiah 55: 12

MARY GAVIN

HOLY SPIRIT

Holy Spirit.
Spark of light
in tongues of fire
or dove so white.

Do me the honour
come dwell in me
and be the torch
with which I see.

Give me courage.
Fill me with peace
so that my love for you
may never cease.

Your strength I need
when I am weak.
When others fail me
Your trust I seek.

Give me the wisdom
to understand God's way.
Take my hand
and lead me today.

In Your presence
a joy I feel
as I know You come
my soul to heal.

John 14: 15-18

MARY GAVIN

LIFE ON THE DOLE

Unemployed
and on the dole.
To get out of that
would be my goal.

Wednesday's dinner –
What will it be?
Omelette and chips
for family and me.

Thursday's a greater challenge.
Checking the edible goods
– alas, again –
It'll be egg and spuds.

Friday - it is
Shopping day.
With the pennies counted
I'm on my way.

I carefully scan
my shopping list.
Sweets and biscuits
will be missed.

To visit friends
I'd love to go
But with empty hands
I'd feel so low.

The door bell goes –
Who's there ? let's see...
In front of me stands
The E.S.B.

Pay up – or else
your supply will be cut.
Here I am
in another rut.

Just pay by cheque
And you'll be spared.
'I don't have an account'
I say real scared.

A night on the town
would be just great
but with nothing to wear
It's not my fate.

Holiday Brochures,
they arrive.
There's not a hope
while we're alive.

The Social Welfare guy
will be our guest
on Thursday next
to conduct a means test.

"If you've got one acre,
a duck, hen or cock,
or a ridge of spuds,
your dole we'll dock"

I scour the papers
a part-time job to find.
Finally I'm in luck,
the contract's signed.

My weekly eighty quid is great,
but Social Welfare do their rounds.
From my husband's dole
they dock fifty pounds.

Psalm 82: 3

'I wrote this some years ago when I was struggling to make ends meet, with five children and a husband on the dole. It's very relevant for many who are in the same situation today.'

The Baton of Faith

From time immemorial
Our Catholic faith
Has been handed on
Like a baton in a relay race
From one generation to the next,
Each being grounded in the rules,
Trained in their practice,
Focused on their implementation
With love and hope and belief
In a greater purpose.

Through famine times
The faith never wavered.
Our ancestors passed on
Our Spiritual inheritance.
Through prayer and strife they did survive.
We owe them a debt of gratitude
Which we can only repay
By treasuring that faith
And passing it intact
To our children.

We owe too, to our relatives
Who died in the effort.
They could have joined another team,
A more prosperous one,
in material terms,
And filled their stomachs
To the loss of their souls.
They lost the battle
But won the race
And received the cup of immortality.

'Now faith is the assurance of things hoped for . . . Indeed, by faith our ancestors received approval'
                    Hebrews 1: 1, NSRVCE

MARY GAVIN, Co. Mayo, Ireland
Mother and grandmother, Mary, is inspired to write poems about life around her, having some published in newspapers and magazines. Mary has written and compiled numerous local history articles for magazines in her local community. Working for over 30 years in Castlebar Library, including 11 years part time, a book she published in 2011 is entitled, '"Mayo Libraries: Memories, tales and anecdotes".

Tomasz Grzymkowski

Proza Życia / Prose of Life

1. Ludzie chodzą zamyśleni, przytłoczeni prozą dnia,
   Wciąż wymyka im się z rąk: radość, miłość, szczęścia smak,
   Tak posępni jak posągi, którym życie rzeźbi twarz,
   Gdzieś biegnący bez wytchnienia,
   Ciągle chcąc wyprzedzić czas.

Ref:
   Zatrzymajmy się na chwilę i otwórzmy serca swe,
   Wyciągnijmy z nich marzenia i zacznijmy spełniać je.
   Zatrzymajmy się w pogoni za przyziemną burzą spraw,
   Zróbmy bilans swego życia, zyski nie pokryją strat.

2. Każdy z nas ma swój cel, do którego dążyć chce,
   Więc szukamy sensu życia, aby nie zatracić się,
   Nasze drogi są tak kręte, niczym rwące nurty rzek,
   Czasem trzeba przycumować, by zobaczyć piękny brzeg.

(Ref)

Tomasz with his wife, Aneta, and son, Alan

Tomasz Grzymkowski

Proza Życia/ Prose of Life

1. People walk lost in thought, writing prose of one's day
   Still slips out of their hands, joy and love, happiness taste
   They are gloomy like statues, faces carved by the life,
   Running somewhere without breath,
   Want to stay ahead of time

Ref:
   Let's stop for a moment and try open our hearts,
   Put the dreams on the top and start making them real.
   Let's stop in the race for the money, glory, gain,
   Give balance to your life, you will lose more than you will get.

2. Every one of us has a purpose in a life,
   We seek a meaning of life, to not lose ourselves,
   Our paths are so winding, like rushing river flows,
   Sometimes we have to moor, to see a beautiful riverside.

(Ref)

Tomasz wrote the song *'Prose of life'* twenty years ago, but recorded it in September 2014 with Irish friends and a Russian girl Diana. Tomasz says, "I wrote this song to say to people that in our life we have more important things than money, career and earnings, and if we're not careful we can lose really important life values".

Tomasz Grzymkowski, Dublin, Ireland
Tomasz was born in Płońsk, a small town in Poland, and grew up in a small village called Strzembowo where his parents have a farm. He is a self-taught musician who always had the dream of writing his own songs and playing in a band. At the age of fifteen, Tomasz began to play guitar and after two years, he and a friend started a band. Tomasz has worked in Dublin since 2007, where he lives with his wife, Aneta, and son, Alan, whom they both agree is the best thing that ever happened to them.

MIKE HARPER

JESUS

In the dark you are my light,
In weakness you are my strength,
In my failure you are my success,
In my prison you are my releaser,
In my distractions you are the one, who shakes me,
In my pride you are the one to humble me,
In my humility you honour me,
In my pain you are my comforter and my healer,
In blindness you are my guide,
When I have no words you are my voice,
When I will not hear anyone your voice breaks through,
In my stubbornness you are patient until the end,
In my treachery you are faithful,
In my sin you still loved me,
In death you are my Saviour,
In disaster you are my redeemer,
In war you are my general,
In love you embrace me,
In the quiet you reveal your secrets to me,
In loud places you calm my heart,
In quiet places you cause me to shout,
In sadness you are my joy,
In joy you are my all,
In brokenness you are my hope,
In friendship you are the best,
In family you are the closest,
Thank you Jesus

Romans 8:35-39

MIKE HARPER

HOLY LAND
(FROM THE ALBUM: PROMISED LAND)

    Wherever I go you are here with me
Wherever you are I will follow you Jesus
          This is Holy Land
        Your grace falls here
       Your mercy falls here
        Your love, your love
        Your love falls here
We lift this land into Your hands
          This is Holy Land
        Your grace falls here
       Your mercy falls here
        Your love, your love
        Your love falls here
   It falls on me, it falls on me

'Look, I am giving all this land to you! Go in and occupy it, for it is the land the LORD swore to give to your ancestors Abraham, Isaac, and Jacob, and to all their descendants.'

Deut 1:8 NLT

MIKE HARPER, DUBLIN, IRELAND

I published my first book as an indie author in early 2012 under the pen name CESAR meaning 'Come Everyone See a Revival'. Since then, I have written several more books giving testimony to what God is doing in my life. I have witnessed many amazing things; visions, dreams and miracles, and some of my experiences I have shared in the books which I have written, in the hope that God can be glorified.

BERNICE HEAPHY

HE DWELLS THERE

There is a place at journey's end
Where we will meet our dearest Friend.
His heart so true throughout each day,
Our hands he holds to lead the way.

He tells me of this glorious land
Where saints and angels walk hand in hand,
Where all life's trials are swept away,
For God is love and He dwells there.

This place of peace, so pure and still,
The saints all sing in joyous thrill,
To see the King upon His throne,
The Lamb of God in our heavenly home.

Oh, what a joy is this to me,
To be with Jesus eternally
And walk and talk with Him every day
In that bright land where Jesus stays.

Come, let us sing of streets of gold,
Of the river of life that flowed of old,
Where the two trees stood in the Garden of Eden,
Where we will return to reclaim our Heaven.

Rejoice, rejoice, this story is told,
That all who come will never grow old,
But live in peace and joy and love
In that bright land with God above.

Isaiah 25: 8

BERNICE HEAPHY

DEAR JESUS

Dear Jesus as I sit here alone and think of You
My heart burns within me for I know You'll be true
You'll always love me, for your words they cannot lie
For you are my God and Your love will not die

I think of the day when I'll see Your wondrous face
I adore You and praise You for Your saving grace
My love for You grows with each passing day
I draw near by Your blood shed on that hill far away

Dear Jesus that I may be able to be
As strong as You want me and be free to be me
For inside me You dwell and the hope that You give
Springs forth from my soul, I shall eternally live

John 17: 3

BERNICE HEAPHY, CORK, IRELAND
Born in Zimbabwe (Rhodesia) in 1941 to Irish immigrants, an alcoholic father and a mother working 2 jobs left Bernice at the mercy of sexual predators who repeatedly abused her from a very young age, causing depression. Supernatural experiences convinced Bernice that God was real. At 16 she asked God to take her from this planet. Visiting heaven, and was filled with complete peace and fulfilment. Some years later, visiting a Pentecostal church, Bernice learned the wonderful news of Jesus dying for her & gave her heart to Jesus without hesitation, assured that one day she would return to heaven to spend eternity with Jesus. Her only desire is to tell everybody that heaven and hell are very real & that Jesus can be their saviour too.

Being the parent of a stillborn girl, I was biblically enraged when I recently learnt about the Cillíní graves. Cillíní are the unmarked graves for unnamed stillborn babies, buried at night, in oft-lonely places. The whole unbiblical concept of "limbo" is a cruel travesty of truth and was a double blow to parents of stillborns in their deep grief...

Cillíní

Hear that hammer hitting, nailing down your sorrow,
your stillborn baby silent, your heavy heart unhallowed,
motherhood murdered, O cruel, poisoned arrow.

O unbaptised baby with such indifferent eyes,
such plaintive questions, kissed tenderly goodbye;
creation heaves, your heavenly Father cries.

Guardian angels quietly watch and weep,
secret graves stubborn spades dig deep,
keening midnight mothers refuse to sleep.

Accursed limbo lies! Sad Cillíní plots moan,
parental pain observed by silent sentinel stones,
sand now pitifully exposes scattered baby bones....

Countless empty arms, countless aching wombs -
there's no human hope to fill such a vacuum;
stillborn babies wait beyond this hopless gloom.

Not 'unknown souls', as clergy wrongly claimed,
all your hairs are numbered, you are newly named,
loved by the heavenly Father, freed from such shame.

Psalm 139: 12-14
from Vimeo video https://vimeo.com/77926614

LOUIS HEMMING, DUBLIN, IRELAND

Louis has been writing for the past 43 years. He has been published in Christian and secular media since the late 1970s. He won The Padraic Colum/Poetry Ireland award in 1981. About 100 of his pithy letters-to-the-editor have also been published in newspapers and online. Louis started writing full time in 2015. His work can be viewed on http://cowbird.com/louis-hemmings/

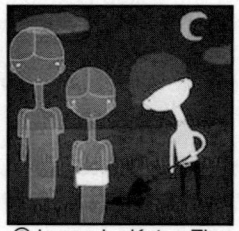

© image by Katya Zhu

LESLIE HOWARD

THRESHING FLOOR

You are the Prince of Peace
You are the Holy Dove
You are my hiding place
Of everlasting love
Be my true heart's desire
Make it your dwelling place
I'm lifted from the mire
By your unfailing grace

Holy God, King of Glory
Took the form
Of a servant, made so lowly
Yet triumphant

Through your redeeming blood
You now have set a seal
Upon believers' hearts
And so we come to kneel
Unto your Throne of Grace
Before the mercy seat
To receive your Power
Salvation words to speak

Oh Holy Spirit
Come to your Threshing Floor and separate
The useless chaff from the chosen wheat
Your Kingdom to take

Alleluia

Matthew 3: 12

LESLIE HOWARD

Lift up the name of Jesus

To whom shall we go Lord, to whom shall we go
You have the words of eternal life
To whom shall we go Lord, to whom shall we go
You have the words of eternal life

Lift up the name of Jesus, Lift up the name of the Lord
Lift up the name of Jesus, Lift up the name of the Lord

Jesus our Prince of Peace
Jesus, our Counsellor
Jesus the Mighty One
Jesus Immanuel

Jesus, the Holy One
Jesus, deliverer
Jesus, the Lamb of God
Jesus, the Lord of all.

John 6: 68

LESLIE HOWARD

THROUGH THE CROWD

Through the crowd bold she went
To touch the hem of his garment
He took her pain away, washed it away
All her pain away, washed it away

You've made your home in me
Healed and set my spirit free
And I am but the clay in your hands
Every single day in your hands

You are The Christ, the only Son
of the living God
The shepherd who's come
To seek the lost
Holy, Holy Lord our God
The angels sing your glory Lord our God

Matthew 16: 16

LESLIE HOWARD

You Alone are God

You alone are God

You alone are Holy

You alone are Wisdom

Everlasting Love

You answered my prayer

When I was in need

When I felt despair

Falling on my knees

Oh the wisdom of my God

How untraceable Your ways

How unsearchable Your judgements

Father, Glory to your name

I thank You from my heart

Though I don't always understand

I want to thank You in my song

Cos in Your victory I stand

John 12: 28

LESLIE HOWARD

MELT THIS HEART

You came to melt this stone
The stone that is my heart
I've come to praise and worship you
King of Kings and Lord of Lords

I humbly come before you Lord
Before Your great and mighty Throne
Come and set this captive free
Come and do a work in me

King of Kings and Lord of Lords

All you that labour and are heavy burdened
Come to me and I'll give you rest

Revelation 19: 16

LESLIE HOWARD, DROGHEDA, IRELAND

Leslie has been writing songs for the past 7 years and has home-produced 4 CDs. Les has also presented 3 concerts in recent years and donates the proceeds of these events to charity. He also frequently facilitates a retreat entitled 'The Divine Plumbline', a course for Christians wishing to reach maturity and come to fuller understanding of their true identity as adopted sons and daughters of the Most High Father God. Les frequently leads the singing at Calvary Christian Fellowship, Bluebell, Dublin.

I'll Soar Like an Eagle

```
     A         A        D       D
I'll soar like an eagle, I'll rest like a dove
     A         A        E    E
I'll carry my dreams on your wings
     A           A      D          D
As we glide through the sky, your joy lifts me high
     A       E       A    A
I will soar like an eagle in your love
```

When structures and restrictions tied me to the earth
You showed me that you have no bounds
And you bid me come and fly with you and to laugh in your mirth
Now no force can keep me on the ground

You flew me over mountains and lakes far and wide
And you showed me the deserts made of sand
You said cos' I'm your child, I'm as free as a bird
For you hold the worlds in your hand.

Isaiah 40: 31

SHIRLEY HOWITT, DONCASTER, ENGLAND

Shirley has sung in Ireland, the United States, India and Britain. Her songs hold very special messages because they are based on lessons that she has learnt, usually through life's very difficult situations. They bring inspiration and comfort to people who are going through emotionally distressing times, finding healing, hope and peace, and a revelation of the God's love, grace and mercy in her songs. As Shirley understands the importance of how the word of God can transform a life, all the songs are based on the word of God. Hear more of Shirley's songs on http://www.shirleyhowitt.co.uk/

CHRISTINE IKWUNWA

NGCWELE, NGCWELE/HOLY, HOLY
(in Zulu/English)

Ngwcele, Ngcwele
(Holy, Holy)   (Lead Singer)
Baba u yi ngcwele
(Father you are Holy)

U yi ngcwele Baba:(Lead Singer)
(You are Holy Father)

Ngwcele,Ngcwele
(Holy, Holy)   (Response) x2
Baba u yi ngcwele
(Father you are Holy)

Hosana :(Lead Singer)

Hosanna u phakeme (Response) x2 (Hosanna in the highest)
Hosanna u phakeme
Hosanna

Matthew 21: 9

CHRISTINE IKWUNWA, CO. CAVAN, IRELAND
Christine, a singer, born and bred in South Africa, moved to Ireland in 2002. Jesus, her Lord and Saviour, is her inspiration in music. Christine is a Gospel singer who believes music evangelizes and inspires people in the word of God. She founded a Gospel Group, Dexi Ministries in Virginia, County Cavan, of which she is lead singer. The group was formed to promote African Gospel and integration amongst Irish people and immigrants through song, ministering and fellowshipping with one another.

RÓISÍN JENKINSON

BOUND

Your bones were broken
while I stood stunned,
looking up at an empty cross.
I could not know,
I could not see
your wrists were bound
in entirety for eternity,
but you broke that chain
of unending time
that now I'm saved, by your side.
Your bones were broken
and could not rebuild
my shattered thoughts of myself.
I sunk without knowing
that you had my hand
to pull me out and see your love
in that Son on that empty cross.
He died there
with wrists and ankles bound,
a thorn crown resting on his head,
blue eyes looking over
our unseeing illusion of independence,
nailed to an empty cross.
Your bones were broken
and now I bleed
for more of your love
to bind my wounds
in this everlasting war
between what's breakable and restored.
Your bones were broken
to shed a light,
now I've been saved
by your graceful guide.

Luke 23:33-34

Róisín Jenkinson

Journey

A blameless breeze carries me through this valley
towards an enchanted, enhanced paradise.
I peer behind me at a flown-away past
where people live in a whirling world, alas.

This world is a twirling twisted tongue-twister
more confusing than the people want to know.
It swallows you to make you believe in them
and not God of all things beautifully born.

A thousand miles ahead Jesus waits for me
to be freed from this dark chamber at long last.
The breeze pushes me onward to golden gate
where my Father's standing with love just for me.

We love because he first loved us.
1 John 4:19 NIV

RÓISÍN JENKINSON

RED

Being surrounded by high rushes and harsh water
as wind lashes at my skin and cold prickles the tips of my ears and nose
causing me to shudder; a shivering being standing in the open
where all can see the truth of my thoughts, leaving me bare, and battling
their remarks and laughter at what they refuse to understand.
With the rushes over my head, I look around and deign to know what they are thinking,
what life they have known and where they come from to make preordained conclusions
without looking more and wondering what this could mean.
Standing alone in these high rushes, with my feet stuck and sinking into the mud,
unable to pull them out, I see in the distance another threat
which causes my face to turn pale and my voice becomes incapable of screaming
for help in this desolate, isolated place, where a beautiful creature of orange
crouches and creeps towards me, waiting for the opportunity
to strike and kill, grabbing my neck in it's teeth and snapping it, dragging my ruined body
up a tree where it tears through my skin to my bones and chews on my carcass.
I struggle to break free from the mud, praying, calling God to rescue me,
crying out and asking why I am here, here in this lonesome isolation
where I stand out like a black blotch on a white wall,
surrounded by iniquity, indecency and misery.
While I am calling, God listens to me and answers me,
comforting me, filling me with his spirit until it's overflowing with a glowing light
and that is when I know, and that is when I feel free of this curse that has been put on me
by the devil and his puppets dangling from thin thread over a pool of red,
some of the feet creating ripples that continue to expand.

That is when I let go, let the tears flow in the presence of the holy spirit and I smile and laugh at this ridiculous gash that pains and torments me,
remembering that God can heal anything no matter how severe, and I laugh again at my own stupidity of forgetting and falling for the threat that hasn't happened yet.
As I stand here with both feet stuck in the mud, surrounded by high rushes,
a tiger crouching and creeping before me, getting ever so closer,
the sound of water filling my ears so all I can hear is white noise,
I shout for God with a voice I cannot hear, stretching my arms out above me
as a child longs for their mother or father to hold them.
I feel a hand close over mine, and holding it tight, they pull me from sinking,
removing me from danger, and hold me in their arms; in their embrace.
The high rushes and harsh water have dematerialised as Jesus holds me now,
his arms wrapped around all of me, keeping me safe and warm,
and I am smiling with tears in my eyes, because I know he is always there for me.

> *So He said, "Come." And when Peter had come down out of the boat, he walked on the water to go to Jesus. But when he saw that the wind was boisterous, he was afraid; and beginning to sink he cried out, saying, "Lord, save me!" And immediately Jesus stretched out His hand and caught him, and said to him, "O you of little faith, why did you doubt?"*
>
> Matthew 14:29-31 NKJV

RÓISÍN JENKINSON

VIVID

Every-so-often
God likes to remind us
of His promises for us.
Sometimes we get so caught up
with what we are doing in the world
that we forget what God has in store.
We need to keep a hold
onto those vivid promises.

'. . . and I will remember my covenant which is between me and you and every living creature of all flesh; the waters shall never again become a flood to destroy all flesh.'

Genesis 9:15 NKJV

RÓISÍN JENKINSON, CO. DUBLIN, IRELAND

Róisín is currently living in Dublin where she is completing a degree course in Fine Art at Dublin Institute of Technology. In her poetry, she seeks to resolve questions she has about everything and to discover more about Jesus. She has three poems published in other anthologies, including a poem in Dan Lake's Electric Winds. She also has an account at allpoetry.com/RoisinJ and a like page on facebook entitled Roisin's Visual Poetry. You can also contact her at roisin.jenkinson@hotmail.co.uk

AMANDA CLARKE

THE HOLY SHOE

Swiftly and spritely the sound of moving feet, through the marketplace along a cobbled street
Onlookers and followers jostle for unbroken view, as they catch a glimpse of a Holy Shoe
Words of truth, healing and strength spoken to multitudes who sit at His command,
Watching the sick healed as He lays down His hand.

Quickly He rises and leaves swift pace, leaving much joy on many a sullen face,
To report to His Father on what He has done, this is proper eticut between Father and Son,
With a heart full of love and eyes full of fire interceeding for others pulling them out of the mire,
Standing regal and in authority with words that divide the purposes of man's heart and what's held inside,

For His name and His blood redeem all who call upon Him who repent and ask for forgiveness of the darkest of sin
Not one does He want to miss with His love and compassion, agape, no conditions that is His fashion,
He welcomes each heart that calls out to cry, when life doesn't make sense and we all reason why,
Looking for completeness to fulfil life's path, not knowing we will come to an end of bloodshed and wrath.

Yet there's a key thats golden and bright, to unlock closed doors and let in the light,
With free choice we can take it and hold it in hand releasing us to go to the promised land,
So when we see a glimpse of that Holy Shoe we must make a choice and follow it too,
For it will lead us to riches and wine of the best, giving us hope, faith and love
With life eternal......His rest.

John 14:6

AMANDA CLARKE

JESUS WITH ME

When times and trials they try to overcome me
I lift my hands my voice to God
For he is my Saviour and my friend ....the one in whom I depend

I praise you Lord
With all my strength
I praise you Lord
For Loving me

Hes still gracious to the humble
The downcast he will exhalt
He gives wisdom to the seeker
The faithful one He will reward

I praise you Lord
With all my strength
I praise you Lord
For Loving me

When I need hope hes there for me
Waiting to comfort and set me free
For hes my saviour and my friend
the one in whom I depend

I praise you Lord
With all my strength
I praise you Lord
For Loving me

I praise you Lord with all my strength
I praise you Lord for Loving me.........
For loving me, for loving me.....
Amen

Psalm 96: 9

AMANDA CLARKE, CO. ANTRIM, N. IRELAND
Irish missionary to Africa, Amanda, demonstrates Gods love in spiritual and practical ways. Pioneering the project 'Circle of Blessing' in rural villages and churches in Uganda and Kenya, she sees miracles, signs and wonders, as new churches are birthed. Preaching, teaching and creativity are part of who Amanda is in the Lord. Returning home to Ireland, she shares her gifting and experiences through prophetic art, poetry and crafts using natural resources. If you would like to know more or support Amanda please log on to www.bigheart.org.uk

CARRIE KELLY

THE FOUNTAIN OF LIFE

The Fountain of Life is a beautiful place ~ it's filled with peace, love and grace ~ there's nothing can take its place
Oh *the Fountain of Life* is a beautiful place

The River of Peace is a quiet place ~ there's nobody there to disturb your pace ~ just the sound of the river as it goes trickling by ~ and the reflection of the pale blue sky
Oh *the River of Peace* is a quiet place

The Rushing Sea is a noisy place ~ it has no manners ~ it'll splash your face ~ it has no patience, it comes roaring in ~ doesn't stay long and goes rushing back out ~ it has no time to hang about~ hasn't time to see who he is taking back to sea ~ if you're on the trip you'll have to wait until he brings you back and throws you out ~ you're all washed up and worn out ~ but it doesn't care ~ it's off again ~ on another journey that never ends
Oh *the Rushing Sea* is a weary place

The Lake of Death is a very still place ~ waiting for you to step out of place ~ it's watching quietly every step ~ waiting and listening ~ it makes no sound ~ you throw a stone in and it drops to the ground ~ no sign of life ~ no cheerful sound
Oh t*he Lake of Death* is a still sound

But the best of all is the Fountain of Life ~ it's bubbling with joy and it's full of life ~ it's on a journey into eternal life ~ it never runs dry ~ it's continually filled ~ it jumps with excitement over every stone ~ one step closer to its eternal home

Oh the Fountain of Life is a lovely place ~ it's the only one going someplace ~the sea goes out and comes back in ~ the river gets lost along the way ~ the lake of death is standing still ~ but the Fountain of Life is running fast ~ a race against time ~ but it won't come last
Oh yes the Fountain of Life is a lovely place!

John 7: 38

CARRIE KELLY

THE ROBOT SOCIETY

No time to chat – no time to care
The robot society is everywhere
They answer the phone in three words – no more – no time to talk anymore
In the robot society where there is no time, your shopping comes racing down a line, can I catch it in time!

Even on the roads they just shoot out at you – no understanding, not even a glace or two, they have a place to be at a specific time and they'll put their life on the line, and anyone else's if they're not on time, the robot society belongs somewhere else, or another planet maybe! Maybe the world doesn't move fast enough for them but it certainly does for me!

I'd like the world to be more patient and kind – more understanding – more tolerant of mind – after all we are only mankind! Listening to people is now very rare, What is wrong – do we not care? The Robot society feels Uncaring and cold, and we all need someone to hold

So why not go back to being people again – and be more caring to men – let the robot society die away and let love come back to stay.

Instead, be kind to each other, tenderhearted, forgiving one another, just as God through Christ has forgiven you.
Ephesians 4:32 NLT

CARRIE KELLY

WORDS

When spoken with love can make you
Feel warm and cozy inside
Words spoken with hatred can send
A shiver of fear right through your spine
Of all the words I've ever heard – the
Judging ones are the worst – when you
Receive a word of encouragement it
Feels like a hundred arms around you
Comforting you like a cloak –the
Judging words are like a cloak of steel,
You feel encased, cold and dead like
The grave

What a lovely gift words can be – used
In the right way – judging words are
Like stones being cast upon you – you are
Being stoned to death by words –
They smother you – and the cloak hangs
Over you for days

> *Kind words are like honey— sweet to the soul and healthy for the body.*
>
> *Proverbs 16:24 NLT*

CARRIE KELLY

The Forest of Life

Life can feel like wandering through a huge forest, lost
And afraid, it feels like you've been there for years.

You don't know your purpose in life, then suddenly you see
The flicker of light, a feeling of hope, you dare to dream
You follow the light, you trudge through bramble and mud
You keep on going even though you feel like crying, your
Bones feel like dying

But your dreams are in your heart
And they've got to come true
No matter how much you go through

It's your existence, your life, the reason you were born
When you're all cut up and all worn out, that is the time to
Shout
I'm not giving in, the forest won't beat me; I'm not turning back

The light will guide me on the right
Track, and one day I'll be there and I can look back
Holding my dream and receiving a pat on the back

Jesus spoke to the people once more and said, "I am the light of the world. If you follow me, you won't have to walk in darkness, because you will have the light that leads to life."

John 8: 12

CARRIE KELLY

THE OLD MAN

I see the old man walking every day –
Dragging his feet along the way
One shoe brown and one shoe grey
His clothes hang from his thinning body
His face is wrinkled and his clothes are
Shoddy
His sadness is visible in his eyes
His loneliness shows in the way he walks
His back is hunched and his head hangs low
I'm wondering where he must go
All I see him do is walk and walk and walk
He lifts his head as I pass by
I catch a glint of happiness in his eye
As I smile and say 'hi'
Then he walks away with his head hung low
And off he walks – where to I don't know

1 Peter 5:7

CARRIE KELLY, CO. MEATH, IRELAND

"I gave my life to the Lord 29 years ago; I was immediately taken from a very dark place of depression and despair to a journey of hope, joy and faith. I am being healed. I started writing poetry to express my overwhelming gratitude to the Lord. I started writing a journal every day, which I still do. I began painting which is very therapeutic, I feel close to the Lord when I paint. I am now writing a memoir to be published in the near future."

WILMA KENNY

THE FATHER'S LOVE

Isolation
was the
    space
society allocated
to me.
Then,
I saw
the heavenly Father.
Felt His warmth
curled around me,
like melted chocolate–
a cappuccino
flavoured
with love.
I drank.
Gulped.
The milky froth of love
    flows
down my eager chin.

Now hope does not disappoint, because the love of God has been poured out in our hearts by the Holy Spirit who was given to us.
Romans 5: 5 NKJV

WILMA KENNY

God Among Us

"Come poets," I called. They came to look at the rhyme,
the weave, the tease of the stories, its unique web and flow
forced them to inquire, "Where can we meet the person
who wrote the book?"

"Come seamstresses," I called. They came and fell to their
knees, stroking the flowers I had gathered, in awe of the
colours, the texture. "Where can we meet the person who
has this eye for detail?"

"Come perfumers," I called; they followed me into the deepest
forest where all the smells of nature mingled. Pine, rambling rose,
wildflower nectar. "This is unique," they screamed. "Bring us
the person who made these."

Finally I said, "Come all you mothers and fathers."
Hundreds of voices gasped. "How can we have such a child?"
They wept at his beauty. Scientists demanded, "Catch the DNA,
make us a unique baby like this."

The poets, the seamstresses, the perfumers, the mothers, the fathers,
the scientists asked, "Who made the patterns, shades, shapes, words?"
I pointed to the baby, "His father. He sent us this baby, his son to help
us to learn how to live in this world."

They all fell to their knees thanking God.

1 John 4: 9, 10

WILMA KENNY

THE MASTER'S SEAL

I am burning
Your love
onto my breast.
Place Your seal on
my life's story.
Melt your wax, Master,
sear it onto my envelope.
Then I shall know You more.

So you are no longer a slave, but God's child; and since you are his child, God has made you also an heir.
Galatians 4: 7 NIV

WILMA KENNY

STRAWBERRY CLOVER

Genesis 1 vs. 11/12
Then God said: "Let the earth produce plants- some to make grain for seeds and others to make fruits with seeds in them. Every seed will produce more of its own kind of plant. And it happened. The earth produced plants with grain for seeds and trees that made fruits with seeds in them. Each seed grew its own kind of plant. God saw that this was all good."

Strawberry clover speaking of God's love
Coral Wort shining forth his beauty
Monkshood telling of divine protection
Elder Orchid rising to worship the creator.
Stone Bramble keeping watch for the master.
Maiden Pink reflecting his glory
Rayless Mayweed the humblest of all
These things whispered to me by the tender stream

WILMA KENNY

HEALING TOUCH

Words hurled in anger bled me
His touch brought healing

I will
Rejoice
Praise
Love

Again
Again
Again

Matthew 9: 21,22

WILMA KENNY, BELFAST, NORTHERN IRELAND

Wilma is an award winning poet and works as a freelance journalist. With husband Andrew, they have two grown up children Andy and Rachel. Wilma enjoy all aspects of the arts especially visual and written. Wilma has found when she is pensive and close to God she writes poems which are in response to her Christian faith. She loves going to literary events such as the John Hewitt International Summer School which she has attended for the past ten years. Wilma has read her poetry on RTE and UCB radio and several years ago was a part of an event at the Edinburgh festival. Many of her poems were written at a residency at Multyfarnham Franciscan Friary.

Spiritual Songs, Poems and Prophecies

DERMOT LANDY

HERE IS MY HEART

Here's my heart, here's my soul,
Here's my life, come take control.
I worship you and you alone, oh God   (x2)

Your nail scarred hands, they pierced your side,
Your crown of thorns, it freed my mind.
I worship you and you alone, oh God (x2)

You bore my pain and iniquity.
You took all sin and died for me.
And now in You, I am free,
So here's my heart and here's my soul.
Here's my life, come take control.
I worship you and you alone, oh God (x2)

My Jesus, my Jesus, I fall at your feet.
Without you, oh Lord, life's so incomplete.
Your every touch to me is so sweet.
The way that you meet my every need,
Only with you do I feel complete.
So here is my heart and here is my soul,
To you, oh Lord, I give control.

Revelation 1: 17-18

DERMOT LANDY, CO. KERRY, IRELAND

Dermot, born into a large family of 12, suffered abuse as a child, physically from an alcoholic father and sexually from a neighbour. Emotionally, he carried the pain of abuse and rejection into adult life. Obsessed with sex, drink and drugs, he attempted suicide, but was rescued. More scrapes with death occurred before Dermot heard the message of a new life: he didn't need to carry his pains and struggles because Jesus had already carried them all at the cross. Dermot began with a fresh start on a rainy Friday evening in March, 2000. He is now married and a leader of a fellowship in Killarney.

VINCENT LYONS

Heart Surgery

Who can know where soul meets spirit?
Who can prise these two apart?
Realm beyond our wisdom's limit
Area no man can chart
Where hides the secrets of the heart.

There, can lurk much pain and sorrow
Fount where thought originates
Deeper far than bone and marrow
Home to unseen hurts and hates
Where sin and trouble incubates.

Man can offer no solution,
Band-aid remedies at best;
Methods based on Truth's dilution
Where man's sin is not addressed
Can never heal the heart oppressed.

Word of God so sharp, incisive
Pierces where dark things may hide
Spirit's Truth so firm, decisive
To the seeking heart applied
Twixt soul and spirit will divide.

Two-edged sword with skilled incision
Cuts to quick where sin infects
Lifts the veil with deft precision,
Source of problem it detects
The power of darkness disconnects.
Quick and pow'rful, sharp and pointed
Word discerns the hearts intent—

Spirit's scalpel, pure, anointed
Will not fail or circumvent—
His lone prescription is—repent!

Glad am I that Heaven's Surgeon
Plied His scalpel to my soul
Excised every sinful burden
Injected life and made me whole—
Now bless the Lord my joyful soul!

> *For the word of God is living and powerful, and sharper than any two-edged sword, piercing even to the division of soul and spirit, and of joints and marrow, and is a discerner of the heart.*
>
> Heb 4:12 NKJV

VINCENT LYONS

FRAMED

Outstanding paintings on display
By the great artist of the day—
Creative works beyond compare;
Astounded thousands stop and stare
At masterpieces hanging there.

The trees, the fields, the lakes sublime
So real I feel that I could climb
Inside the frames and be a part
Of these amazing works of art;
Such is the feel his works impart.

Through shade and colours brilliant use
The world I know is reproduced

I stand and gaze in awe, admire
These works that lift my senses higher
To worship Him Whose works inspire.

In halls of learning he's acclaimed;
By everyone of note he's named,
Throughout the world he's recognised,
His paintings are so highly prized
His fame's become immortalized.

How prone we are to venerate
Mere men whose best works imitate
Unrivalled masterpiece of One
Whose art can never be outdone
Whom art and art-world often shun?

So step inside the world God framed,
See brilliance everywhere proclaimed;
Experience His art first hand
Give Him the praise His works demand;
Acclaim His fame o little man!

Psalm 19:1

VINCENT LYONS

INTERTWINED

Faith, hope and love when intertwined
Release us from the cords that bind;
When these combine as three in one
There's nought can bring the soul undone.

Faith must come first, the centre piece
Fed by His Word its strands increase
In strength to carry through each doubt—
All fabrications must get out!

Where faith is certain, hope controls,
It weaves itself through heart and soul
Each aspect of our life renews,
Anxiety and fear excludes.

Such faith and hope now formed within
Bears witness to the world of men;
What Christ has done in changing me
Through love outworking, others see.

Love is the strand God's Spirit weaves
Through which the world at large perceives
The mighty change that God has done
In one now trusting in His Son.

Faith, hope and love are intertwined
A threefold cord that God designed;
His Spirit braids each strand in place
A work of His amazing grace.

1 Cor. 13:13

VINCENT LYONS, AUSTRALIA
"I was born in County Galway and came to Australia in 1974. I have always enjoyed writing poetry, and after becoming a Christian in 1985, I decided to try my hand at writing from a purely biblical perspective. Obviously it is a work in progress, and as I progress in my knowledge of Christ, hopefully my poetry will become more inspired and beneficial to others. I also like to write light hearted verse as a form of escapism."

THOS MAHER

THE GREY HERON

In the shallow water
There sweeps a cold wind
A lone heron hangs out
And boldly stalks a fish,
Or an eel maybe
It feels that is there,
Then with startling speed
It pricks its prey.
Death – so sudden
But winter has come.
Still, when all is done
And happy with its lot
This gaunt bird
Arches its wings
And is silently away.

*I know all the birds of the air,
 and all that moves in the field is mine.*

Psalm 50: 11 NRSVCE

THOS MAHER, COUNTY KILDARE, IRELAND
Thos is a native of Urlingford, County Kilkenny. He works in public transport in Dublin, and lives in County Kildare with his wife and daughter. Thos has been dabbling in poetry for years and likes making up verse in his spare time. 'The Grey Heron' first appeared in a CIE Anthology named 'It Happens between Stops', September 2010, and later, in the Galway Review on-line in December 2012.

CAILIN NÍ THALLÚIN

SAY 'NO!' TO 'GAY-MARRIAGE'

Dear Father God,
Protect our family tonight –
Don't let it be corroded by the devil's bite.
Attacking it from every angle –
Abuse, divorce, abortion,
Now we hear a 'Gay Marriage' jangle.

Protect our children from lies of the enemy –
'Unsure of your sexuality' they say,
'Experimenting is the remedy'.
God forgive us for not praying more!
Do we not understand 'liberty to sin'
Gives lawlessness an open door!

Protect our hearts, Lord.
"Love the sinner, hate the sin."
But to condone their sin we cannot afford.
For every law made, we reap the consequences.
Help us to make godly choices –
From evil pursuit, maintain high defences.

Eph 5: 2-7 NKJV

News 2015 – A referendum in the Republic of Ireland as to whether 'gay marriage' should become part of constitutional law is to be held on May 22nd (after this book has gone to print). Meanwhile, Asher's Bakery in Northern Ireland, owned by Christians, was taken to court on March 26th by a gay-activist for refusing to bake a cake inscribed with the slogan, 'Support Gay Marriages'. The judge 'reserved' her decision in order to gather more information about the case. Thousands met at Waterfront Hall, Belfast, ahead of the hearing, to show support to Asher's Bakery.

Cailin Ní Talamh

WATER, WATER, EVERYWHERE

Water charges everywhere.
Don't pay, if you dare,
Or should you pay to Caesar what's due? –
Hefty levies, so what's new!

2015 News – Ireland's government introduce water charges to residential homes. Ireland is strongly divided on the subject, some believing the charges are fair, whilst thousands refuse to pay and demonstrate to protest.

BRENDAN MARRETT

THE GHOST OF THE UNSAID

Car horns beep.
All people gossip – all –
The world keeps turning, turning.
I disappeared and no one noticed.

The boy endured another hellish day at school and at home –
Not hellish in the painful sense;
His ache was of a desensitised nature.
Every second: Stabbed, skewered with numbing needles that
Anaesthetised his soul and stripped him of sensation.
No, his life was far from hellish – it was art.
He had been created, yet did not live; only existed.
He was an image: a perpetually ignored frost-encased statue gathering dust.
He had been moulded and disregarded like an unfashionable piece of art.
It took all he had to keep his head above water.

Undressed he stared in the mirror.
The large reflected nose risked poking the authentic boy in his
Two owl eyes,
Brown, the shade of a mushed autumn leaf –
The season when things die.
They appeared to quiver, as if to cry,
But he would never let that happen.
Though seemingly feeble, he was strong
Enough to suppress every emotion
That threatened to leak out of his body.
Happiness, melancholia, pain, terror, rage,
All contained, because this is the perfect state.
Emotions are dangerous things. Thus,

Repression was his speciality.
Admitting defeat: Never an option.
Asking for help:
Talking is only a sign of strength
Until your words are used against you.

The white box filled with steaming water.
Bobbling bubbles oozed oily.
Empirical snowy mountains rose from the deep lake
As did citric steam.
When the bath was quite full,
Water scalded toes bold enough to dip in.
It was painful,
But at least it was a feeling.

Succumbing to the desperation
He ran a hand through his hair, white with crust.
He had spent some time that morning meticulously
Combing buckets of dandruff from his scalp, a magnet for dead skin,
But sit in front of a sniggering fat ginger and a tiny twig armed with correction fluid
And these things happen.

Before climbing in, he examined his masculinity
And saw what he felt most ashamed of.
It was everywhere.
It was natural, sure, but why did it have to grow on his body?
He was the shortest guy in his year group, yet his body was the most developed
And horrid.
He wanted to peel away this life and emerge as someone new and pastless and free.

The bathroom window was closed, forcing
Floods like horses to run down the tiled walls.
Blinding vapour encircled the entire room.
The door and neatly folded clothes resting atop his spotless runners vanished.
Nothing was left, but
A misted scene and mysterious mind.
The top of the bath had two metal handles opposite each other.

His arms bent like swan necks from the bubbly blanket and grasped
them tight.
His body rested beneath the water that scorched his face and whatever
else remained of him.

He had always expected his life to flash before his eyes
Before he died.

But he found forcing his consciousness through the canals of his mind
harder than expected.
All he could think about was the world outside the window
– The one he had believed he'd been destined to change –
Which he'd never see again
If he faded away.

Time passed.
Beneath the effervesce surface he lay
Invisible to all but the eyes of God.
No one would see him if they tried.
After embarrassingly long he realised
He had forgotten to take a deep breath –
He had just shut his mouth and
Disappeared
And lay
There.
The soles of his feet shrivelled.
His arms began to tire.
Their hold on the sides of the bath
Weakened.
He had already decided to let go
Of all that he was
And all he had been through
And all he would have been
And all he had had to put up with
And all the things he had never told
And would never get the chance to
When something happened he had not expected:
A thought!

Is this how it ends?

An exposed corpse hogging the only bath in the house,
The door locked?
This is it? This is a life?
Is this how I want to be remembered?
No.

His hands slipped,
And he was offered up to the world without end.

And so it was:
He escaped the snowy sarcophagus, dried himself, and
Powdered so much he became the colour of the bath;
His ghostly body a reflection of the near-death.
No one had the wit to know what happened,
Inert before the television
To the splashing
And the kicking
And the squeaking of fingertips
As he pushed against the walls of
An above-earth coffin.
No-one knew and
No-one was going to know.
That which haunted him
And protected his secrets
Would not want him to
Feel better.
He turned the key, turned off the light, and went to
His room.

But before this,
He opened the bathroom window.
The threatening, steamy shroud of the air within
Whirled close to the lintel,
Just for a moment, menacingly, reluctant to leave,
And then
Disappeared.

(From 'The Ghost of the Unsaid', Brendan's soon-to-be published novel)

1 Kings 18:3-5

BRENDAN MARRETT

WHEN ALL THIS IS OVER

When all this is over,
I will be free to wake – without wishing I still slept.
I will be free to smile – without being told it's ugly.
I will be free to laugh – without it being thought odd.
I will be free to joke – without feeling I've bored them.
I will be free to walk – without being ambushed.
I will be free to play – without being called gay.
I will be free to achieve – without being wished dead.
I will be free to excel – without being told I have no worth.
I will be free to live – without dreaming that I'm drowning.

Romans 5: 1-5

OH, YES PLEASE

After Dennis O'Driscoll's 'No, Thanks'

"Why yes, I would love to borrow your mother's books on crime, medieval heroes, and wolves. It's not like I've waited nine months to leisure read *The Hunger Games* trilogy for the fifth time."

"You've baked muffins? With raisins? My favourite! Pity though, I've just brushed my teeth."

"You've insulated your attic? You kept that a secret, you sly dog, you. Lead the way!"

"A shirt? For me? Wow, I've never seen that shade of grey before. Or is it green?"

"Yes, that *Yakult* sample was just so Yakulty that I insist on buying two dozen."

"Well, I have just begun writing a paragraph on the many faces of Hamlet in 'The Nunnery Scene', but of course I'd love to go do your photocopying – it's not like it's in your job description."

"Summer reading? A part-time job? Learning how to drive? Now, now, how could I even consider the likes, when I can have so much fun mixing a bucket of cement as your husband tiles that garage-cum-utility room you can't stop telling the neighbours about?"

"Yes, you did predict obesity in my future. That said, I don't hold grudges, and I would love nothing more than that chocolaty ensemble of empty calories you bought in *Lidl*."

"Of course I want more cabbage. Who doesn't just love cabbage? And turkey? You are positively spoiling me. My... favourite... member of the poultry family! – Sure, you offer him chicken."

"Watch the football? With you? For a whole ninety minutes? What an honour! I don't deserve it. I really don't. Really."

"Oh, yes please, yes please, mega-deadly-awesome yes please. Sure why even ask? You obviously know me, oh so well."

> ..."Why did you come down here? And with whom have you left those few sheep in the wilderness? I know your pride and the insolence of your heart ...
>
> *1 Samuel 17: 28 NKJV*

(Eliab, casting his ridiculous aspersions on his youngest brother David, regarding his presence among the forces of Israel prior to the death of Goliath.)

BRENDAN MARRETT

INTERPRETATIONS

After Mourid Barghouti's 'Interpretations'

A pair of shifty eyes sits in the canteen,
Phone in hand.

The shy boy thinks
She's scary.

The teacher thinks
Penalty sheet.

The up-and-coming Queen Bee thinks
Idol.

The X-Men fan thinks
Emma Frost, the White Queen.

The bloggers think
E-bullying.

The Special Needs assistant thinks
She's insulting the autistic students.

All surprised
When she rises,
Gives her friend a hug,
Says, "'s okay,"
And tells her to
Forget him.

1 Samuel 16: 7

BRENDAN MARRETT

THE SCARECROW, A SONNET

Black Vs hover overhead, vulturous hunger in their eyes, then
Conceal their faces with coaly clouds from the grim sight:
A winding spiked crown *shunks* into its
Lopsided pumpkin face, so swollen it swallows its own pitch eyes.
Its withered limbs, void of the strength the elements stole yet never
more magisterial.
Choked as if by serpents are wrapped ropes around its hands and feet,
and they
No more than straw, thin, wet, yellow, red.
Its body, but a pole, emaciated and damp, has a look of fetor about it,
Much like the stained, tattered garments that clutch to its feeble, limp
Carcass.

Butchered, it hangs in shreds
Nailed to a tree, a little sign above its head
That reads:
JESUS OF NAZARETH, THE KING OF THE JEWS.

Deuteronomy 21: 22-23

BRENDAN MARRETT, COUNTY LOUTH, REPUBLIC OF IRELAND

An avid writer since he first saw "The Lord of the Rings: The Fellowship of the Ring", Brendan is a twenty-one year old MA English student and aspiring novelist. When not writing essays, he can be found reading Shakespeare in one of his "The Hunger Games" t-shirts, or deciding what episode of "Desperate Housewives" to watch while dreaming he's in an episode of "Buffy"- unless, of course, he's busy concocting his most recent "Pretty Little Liars 'Who Is A?'" theory over a cup of tea.
Contact: brendanthomas94@hotmail.com

Lynne Mary-Lou

The Eyes to See

"The invariable mark of wisdom is to see the miraculous in the common." Ralph Waldo Emerson

God uses the people of this world that are despised, rejected and common to dumbfound the intelligent.
Why you may ask?
So no man shall boast yet give all glory and honour to Him.

I've seen the miraculous in the common every day, not alone the things we tend to take for granted, which are off course all miraculous. Yet to be privileged to witness and experience healings... my own healing of being cured of word blindness or dyslexia, my first son's healing of demonic spiritual attachment for the first three years of his life...three years of sleepless nights and prayer healed over night!

Many wonderful events in the everyday common situation were transforming my life, my faith, and my character.

The most miraculous of all events was when God used a common Jewish girl from a place where everyone said, "What good can come out of Nazareth" to bring the Saviour of the world into our lives.
Poor and common, despised and rejected

Nonetheless, miraculous was Gods' plan for mankind for those who have the wisdom to see.

Luke 1: 34-35

LYNNE MARY-LOU

NOBBY

Nobby was my little brother
However he was driven mentally insane
There wasn't a thing I could do
To stop the torturer the mental pain

Oh Nobby I am so sorry
That you were born to be a boy
To be toughened up
For my parents to destroy

Punch after punch blow after blow
From a boxer in the army
Daddy beat you up
Into an emotional tsunami

So when you grew up
You flipped your wig
Beating up everyone
You felt really big

Your wife and three daughters
Had to go into hiding
Yet her dad was the only one
She could confide in

Bashing on his door
Shouting "where's my f***ing wife"
Threatening the old man
With a petrol chainsaw knife
Smashing up his van
By ramming yours into his

Terrifying the neighbours
And your own kids

The hatred that was in you
Wouldn't allow you any peace
Until your father-in-law
Lifted the shotgun
And the double barrel he released

He blew away your head
While you were rolling a cigarette
Outside a London police station
Without a single regret

He received two years sentence
Cos he was provoked beyond all doubt
I visited him in prison
With cigarette papers and some snout

I just wanted to hear his story
Letting him know I bare no grudge
To bring him my forgiveness
As God is the only judge

He may have pulled the trigger
Of that double barrelled gun
Yet who loaded the ammunition?
Yes my dad and my mum...

For if you forgive people their trespasses (their reckless & wilful sins, leaving them, letting them go & giving up resentment), your heavenly Father will also forgive you.

Mat 6:14 Amp

LYNNE MARY-LOU

TAKING ALL THE CREDIT

I often pray for miracles
For I know my God is great
I prayed that God would fix my van
And my problems alleviate

He hears my prayer and answers them
Because he is so good
From the automatic transmission
To the engine under the hood

It could have cost me thousands
Yet His mercy He does show
To keep my little van running
And help my faith to grow

Yet I really feel frustrated
When my friend explains it all away
Exclaiming the vehicle just fixed itself!
It's God he does betray

He nullifies the faith and hope
That people have in their hearts
He lowers their expectations
And seeds of doubt he imparts

When I pray and give my gratitude
People look as if I'm mad
For giving God the credit
I find that really sad

My friend tried to take the credit
And the glory upon his head
For a previous time there was a leak
Not glorifying God instead

All good things come from God
And He often uses folk
To answer prayer upon this earth
Furthermore His Spirit, we actually evoke

Every good and perfect gift is from above, coming down from the Father of the heavenly lights, who does not change like shifting shadows.

James 1: 17 NIV

LYNNE MARY-LOU

How He Makes My Heart Delight

As I awoke recalling my dream
With words echoing from above
"LEAVE, before circumstances force you to leave"
An assertive message with power and love

For this was no ordinary dream
Left with an image of our new abode
It was a prophetic message
As I was assured the school is just down the road

Now to make haste and search the web
For I knew our Father had reserved us a palace
Ushering His children to safety
Protecting us from instability and malice

Oh how I delight in my Heavenly Father
As He delights so much in me
He's so gracious and so caring
From the enemy always setting us free

Our home is a dream house
Only God could find us this place
Waking up to see the sunrise
Looking upon His almighty grace

Why does He love me so much
And tend to all of my wishes
And so lavishly favours me
With such heavenly riches?

What husband could compete?
With a Father so rich and noble?
Could I ever find a spouse
In this country or even global?

My Father sets the measure
Of how we should be treated
When He sends a true Christian spouse
My family can be completed

For we can serve Him throughout our lives
Until we breathe our very last breath
Rejoicing and worshiping Him forever
For in Him there is no more death

His son made it all possible
By dying on the tree
Uniting us with His Father
For all eternity

Matthew 1: 13-14

LYNNE MARY-LOU, IRELAND

Lynne trained as a bereavement counsellor and listening ear for the bereaved by suicide. She concentrates mainly on expressive writing and encourages others to work through their pain, anger sorrow & bewilderment through therapeutic writing to bring about peace & healing...

Lynne is dyslexic & has experienced heavenly and ongoing healings throughout her traumatic life. Although dealing with many serious subjects, Lynne can quite often have a burlesque SoH and still has a refreshing, childlike trust in her Creator.

Contact: Bethshebha@gmail.com

Anne McCracken

Saying Goodbye

Shadowed room glowing fire and you
    Still ornaments curtained window too
        Green gardens faraway grey sky
            Lonely windblown tree
        Sighing wind rustling leaves
    Darkness falling fading footsteps
Smell of your perfume in quiet house

A little while, and you will not see me; and again a little while, and you will see me . . . Therefore you now have sorrow; but I will see you again and your heart will rejoice, and your joy no one will take from you.

John 16: 16, 22 NKJV

ANNE MCCRACKEN

THE AWAKENING

On a dim dark day at winter's end
The tall bare branched trees are silhouetted
Starkly against the pale sky.
Winter has been like a sleep: lifeless, dull and heavy,
But now, far below the cold brown earth,
Little plants & flowers begin to stir
And prepare to burst through the ground.
Those in hospital begin to improve.
The young await the future.
The old await life's end and its trials.
For what is there worth holding on to
Compared with Eternal Life.....

My beloved spoke, and said to me:
"Rise up, my love, my fair one,
And come away.
For lo, the winter is past.
The rain is over and gone.
The flowers appear on the earth . . ."
                Song of Solomon 2:10-12 NKJV

ANNE MCCRACKEN, CO. ANTRIM, IRELAND

Anne grew up under the artistic and literary influence of her late father, mother and extended family. Anne's parents came from humble, yet large and influential families, acquainted with laughter and joy, and were characteristic of generations who regularly gathered together for fun, laughter and sing-alongs.

Susannah McCracken

SHINE ON BRIGHT SPIRIT

She is beautiful sitting in her own graceful way
Hidden beneath a grubby old blanket that soon becomes transparent
As I look with eyes to see, her bright spirit shines through the smoke
As she softly hums to herself, always believing the good, I see clearly...
Love, to her, never fails, is infinite, irreplaceable and buried deep within.
Her faith in love is unshaken, although life splashed deep despair
Unshaken and solid as an anchor to the rock Christ Jesus.
Holding tightly amidst the dark shadows, the key to everlasting hope.
Deep within her heart abides pure beauty, invisible to some
who may not yet see with their heart, but to her heart, Love never fails.
And those who cherish unconditional love will be awakened.
I love my mother, her fair spirit a priceless legacy to my soul.

But let your adorning be the hidden person of the heart with the imperishable beauty of a gentle and quiet spirit, which in God's sight is very precious.

1 Peter 3:4 NKJV

SUSANNAH McCRACKEN

REBELLION

What you doing, Rebellion
Can't you see this pride is spurring you on?
You've got your eyes fixed in all the wrong places
Always trying on different faces
What you doing, Rebellion
Can't you see it's just selling you on
Deceptions going in deeper and deeper
Obstacles in your soul getting steeper and steeper.

What spell are you under
All those whispers in your ear came subtly while in despair
Now you're caught up in misconception and a slave to the whole affair
Let go of delusions and spread your wings
Receive salvation that will fulfil your dreams
Your soul could dance, flooded by incorruptible Spirit
Overcoming corruption with the one who's already defeated it.

Do you think you could never be deceived?
Within this deception, pride will breed
Don't be fooled by twisted perception, humble yourself, give it no reception
Don't be subject to subtleties of fear, to the Master of the universe you're designed to adhere. Come on Rebellion you've just got to see within corrupt parameters true love could never be
You really want to go somewhere
And through Eternal scope you've got so much to share
Covered and defined within the Eternal, you'd be released into so much more...
Your Life could be so sweet and honey lemon
If you'd just stop selling your soul.

Proverbs 11:2

Susannah McCracken

THE UNCREATED ARRIVES
HE IS THE LIGHT AND BELIEVERS ARE HIS MULTIFACETED DIAMONDS.

Darkness

Barren Emptiness

The Uncreated Arrives

Eternally Bringing

Light.

In the beginning God created the heavens and the earth. The earth was without form, and void; and darkness was on the face of the deep. And the Spirit of God was hovering over the face of the waters. Then God said, "Let there be light"; and there was light. And God saw the light, that it was good; and God divided the light from the darkness.

Genesis 1: 1-4 NKJV

SUSANNAH McCRACKEN

AWAKENING THE SLUMBERING BRIDE

Somewhere behind, lie frozen parts of me.
Moments gone, yet living on in elusive resonance
A smoky existence
Where hidden cries and broken hope sleep
Occasionally they stir and peep
Is it safe to come out and die that I might live?

Bittersweet sounds echo
Love longing to know
The touch of warm fingertips calling to life a slumbering bride
Playing music to her frozen spirit through trembling skin
Warm lips kissing long lost tears from sleepy eyes.

Here he comes, El Shaddai
The Holy One of Israel who will never die
Breathing over nations, awakening his bride
Calling her to respond, to stand by his side

The Bride Awakens from a slumbering daze
Frozen hearts melt within his fiery blaze
Kissed by the King, blood-bought hearts are redeemed
His warm touch healing, meeting deepest needs
His presence releases vision and fulfilment of dreams.

Isaiah 54: 5

Susannah McCracken

I DREAMED A DREAM

I dreamed of two places distinguished by smells of essences of things not easy to tell..... Like a feeling I got in an impersonal room.....
The contrasting essence between upheaval & what I knew to be good.
There a sour smelling atmosphere lingered in the air like gone off milk.

"There I looked in", at the detail of benches by a lonely back door.....
Wondering how for a decade this shallow place had been called home.
I stood there perplexed with my aching heart expecting more.
Expecting to recognise something warm and sure.....
Yet feeling distanced.....Wronged..... like we could never really belong.

Yet dreamy distant glimmers trickled through of sweet remembrance of belonging we once knew.....Of marmite smells, pot belly laughs
And wrinkled smiling faces.....Of well worn chairs and familiar faces.....
Helicopter sounds and cooing birds in the sunny summer garden.....
And even in winter, always seeing the reassuring hills rising
Through the smoky Belfast air.

Remembering the gentle, quiet Granny who showed us love, tucked us in at night and taught us how to care.....Of a strange and funny neighbour who from her window in the daytime loved to stare.....
Of the tender loving Granda with the pot belly laugh who encouraged me to sing, make music, dance and pray. Humorously he would point the neighbour out and offer her a jolly triumphant wave.....

It was then that warm smells of joy flooded when finding the pot belly stained glass maker singing, with ears to hear and eyes to see he created masterpieces, catching rays of sun shining through coloured pieces.....Turning darkness to light.....as he captured what his spirit saw.....Thoughtful and imaginative in his peaceful green shed.....
Smiling as his little ones entered.....With his welcoming eyes poised over thick 50s style glasses upon his adorable shining silver head.
He had colourful bits 'n' bobs scattered.
Curiously, through mysterious drawers and cupboard spaces.....
Tools and digging spades, for the earthy soil that he became.

"Later," the cold wood on the lonely benches, where the sour smelling air stifled my senses, in that distant place..... And now dreaming, of standing in the threshold of a gaping back door.....
Noticing it in stark contrast, to the "then" welcoming,
but now fading glimmering hope I once knew.....
And now I long to grasp once more the essence of that place where the depth of glowing warmth and the marmite smell lingered, at home!
Reminding me endlessly that things would always be well.....
And now the gleanings of their tender love seem like distant dreams.
.......And I weep.......

Yet I know that I know that we and their soul belongs with God
.......So nothing is as it seems.......
As for me and my blood line, I know the Blood of Christ will incline.
As He works all together for good.

Romans 8: 28

SUSANNAH MCCRACKEN, CO. ANTRIM, IRELAND
Susannah was grounded under the artistic and literary influences of family members. In her twenties and thirties Susannah realised her own unfolding creativity to write, and also developed as a singer/song writer. Susannah attributes this to the abiding presence of the Holy Spirit operating in her life.

GERALDINE McDAID

CARING HANDS

From a young age, I had caring hands,
Supporting my Nana as she struggled at night,
With stooped body to make bathroom visits.
The eldest of seven children, I held my sibling's hands
To usher them across a busy Clarendon Street in Derry.

Later, in Nursing, my hands bathed many a brow in sickness,
Anguish, fear and delirious with fever.
In Midwifery, my hands safely guided precious ones
Into this busy world,
Honoured to have participated in that first journey of birth,
And share in a couple's happiness, in most cases.

These hands held my own children-precious jewels,
As my husband shared with me the biggest responsibility of all
Parenting-no mean task!
These hands have more to do, and in God I trust
     He'll guide me all the way.

Colossians 3: 12

HOME

Stony country house,
My comfort, loved refuge,
Envelopes precious ones.

Proverbs 9: 1

Jessie

JOHN MCDAID

WHY?

As I eat this bread
I thank God I'm
alive

As I drink this tea
I thank God I'm
alive

As I hear of all the
distress in the world
I ask God Why?

Then I hear the news and I know
Why

Man still does not love
As You do
Why? Oh why? Oh why?

John 15: 12

JOHN & GERALDINE MCDAID, CO. MEATH, IRELAND

John and Geraldine, originally from Northern Ireland, live in and run a retreat centre in Stamullen, Co. Meath, called Rathnacarach (Irish) meaning 'Way of the Sheep'. John's background is in catering management, while Geraldine's is in nursing. In June 2013 Geraldine had an opportunity to do a poetry and photography course in Dundalk, writing her two poems then. John decided to try his hand in writing his first poem for this book. They have three grown up children - Fearghal, Niamh and Ruairí, and an adorable dog called Jessie!

Contact: johnrakeeragh@eircom.net

LYDIA MCDOWELL

WHO IS HE

Who is this Holy Shining One
so far away from my boxes,
making a space that is a
tumult among the order of my life?
Who is He,
that sits so serenely on a throne
I've never seen,
made of sapphire and flames?
He walks and talks like glowing,
growing, changing, louder.
Who is He? Who is He?
How does He know me?
Do I know Him?
This Lovely One, with a face of Gold
and many stars within his eyes,
even when I see none around us to reflect them?
Who is He in the beauty of His suffering?
I see so much glory in His pain,
how did this come to Be?
Who is this Shining One
that waits with a forever patience on my words?
Who is He,
in glory and love, making spheres around me
that protect me?
Who, is this Lord among all lords,
reaching out of the stars and heavens
to bring me to see His world?
Who is He that would look at
me and say
Hello.
We've met before,
and I love you.

Lydia McDowell

You Are Mine

You can do nothing
that I cannot do,
believing your river
flows all the way through
My heart and your garden
and the songs that are new
creating a space
for you to breakthrough,
I love you I love you Oh darling of mine;
Give Me your heart, your mind and your time
and I'll give you the world as our palms intertwine
the source of this goodness: yes, Me and Mine,
and the angels will dance like stars in your eyes
and batting the lashes of your future life;
they're dislodging the kisses, falling like wine
into the future where you're set to shine.
Child of hope, My son. Yes! You're Mine.

Song of Songs 6: 3

Lydia McDowell, Co. Down, Northern Ireland
Lydia McDowell is a young poet and artist. Her inspiration comes from experiences with Jesus that began in very early childhood as dreams and visions have always been part of her life and Heaven has always felt close. The ancient Celtic mysticism of Ireland has influenced much of her life and inspired her art. She is currently taking a gap year after finishing her A-levels to connect more deeply with the Lord before pursuing art at university.

EMMA LOUISE MITCHELL

TOM

Forty Six Years at the shipyard,
A mammoth achievement that was.
By today's standard of loyalty,
None could compare or come close.

You were always on top of your job there,
You never allowed any slack.
The way you conducted your trade there,
Was with pride, precision and knack!

The alarm would wake the whole house up,
We groaned and knew it was you,
Once again on your way to the shipyard,
Come rain or sunshine blue.

The noise of the car engine revving
Nearly drove us insane at the time,
But sure, you were only getting ready,
Into work again you would sign.

The days they seemed to be endless,
No change of routine or attire,
The same old Overalls worn,
Lunchbox under the arm.

So teach us to number our days, that we may apply our hearts unto wisdom.

Psalm 90: 12 KJV

EMMA LOUISE MITCHELL

HARLAND & WOLFF

From my bedroom window
 as far as the eye could see
Two yellow cranes stood tall
 as you look out toward the East
Landmarks of the City
Landmarks of the Quay,
 where so many ships were built,
 and launched in the Irish Sea.

The early morning taskforce
 were up before daylight,
On their way to "The Yard",
On the bus? not a seat in sight!
Heavy Coats and Caps were worn
 to keep out the morning dew,
Frost and Snow were always the lot that fell,
 especially upon you!

The dark and dismal mornings
 seemed gloomy once again,
But soon cheered up
 when friends met up
 with a nod, cap tossed, "how are you?"

For he looked for a city which hath foundations, whose builder and maker is God.

Hebrews 11: 10 KJV

Emma Louise Mitchell

The Final Launch
January 24th 2003

The final launch of the very last ship
Takes place from the Quay.
An Era's End is marked today,
When it's over we will see,
How much Harland & Wolff
Meant to you and me

Part of our existence
Taking note unconsciously
We've seen those cranes from the side of our eye,
No matter where we'd be.
To a teenager who didn't care,
To the Apprentice who trained there,
It's in the memory of us all
With its memoirs of Titanic's despair.

In the 1970s
The bustling Industry thrived,
The throng of men embarking
Toward the Shipyard skyline.
The sights and sounds of men at work,
All valuable - every one,
Their individual tasks fulfilled
With meticulous detailed sum.
No slack allowed in this business,
When lives would be at stake
Reputations on the line,
No risks prepared to take.
With every launch a standard held
Which spoke of commitment and purpose
To present the finished product
Confident of service.

Safe in the knowledge that all was done,
With fingertip precision,
The Ships were launched into the Irish Sea
With satisfactory resolution.

At least within our memory,
We can still hold close what's dear,
But changes come, we have to accept,
 and still we carry on.
New plans in place for the Shipyard
I wonder what they'll be
Will they come to fruition?
Time will tell you and me.

> *To everything there is a season, and a time to every purpose under Heaven....and a time to Cast Away.*
>
> *Eccl 3: 1 KJV*

EMMA LOUISE MITCHELL, MULLINGAR, IRELAND
Emma, born in Belfast in 1961, is a lover of life and lover of the Creator who has blessed us through His Son with blessings beyond measure and imagination! Her poems are in remembrance of her Stepfather, Tom Law, who worked his whole life at the Harland & Wolff Shipyard in Belfast. They are written as she looks back on a childish perspective, and surrenders her everyday emotions into the hands of God, who holds true perspective, as HE WHO IS, WAS, AND IS TO COME. Amen!

ROSALEEN McGUINNESS

DARK NIGHT OF THE SOUL

There's a certain kind of loneliness
That seems to take control
No matter how bright a day may be
Darkness pervades the soul

It's a loneliness of spirit
That can't or won't respond
To any outside influence
As though it's gone beyond

Saints call it 'dark night of the soul'
For many it's a trial
When God, it seems, abandons us
Forever, or a while

Like a game of hide and seek
Finding God becomes a quest
Do you trust Him above all things?
Will your faith withstand the test?

Christian life is not plain sailing
Much will leave us at a loss
But Oh the privilege of sharing
Just one splinter from the cross

Psalm 27: 7-9

ROSALEEN MCGUINNESS

CONNEMARA HEALING

Raw was the pain of my grief
Matched only by the raw beauty
Of this wild place
A beauty, which at the appointed time
I would learn to accept as sheltering arms
Enfolding all my heartache
Many days were spent in sorrowful haze
Aimlessly walking in chosen solitude
Your silent hills
Many nights the Connemara wind
Hushed my fretful spirit to sleep
Grief pays little tribute to its setting
Yet now that I have broken through
The darkness of the journey
I thank the Lord for the peace
That I have found in these healing
Connemara hills

Blessed are those who mourn, for they will be comforted.
Matthew 5: 4

ROSALEEN McGUINNESS

DO NOT BE AFRAID

Lord to You
I submit the anxiety in my life
When I dwell in the past
Remind me that Your grace
Is offered for Here and Now
Not for There and Then
When I'm tempted
To fast-forward the future
Dear Lord distract me
With Your blessings
No matter how high
The wave of panic
In my personal storm
Let me always hear
Your comforting words
"Do not be afraid"

Do not worry about anything, but in everything by prayer and supplication with thanksgiving let your requests be made known to God. And the peace of God, which surpasses all understanding, will guard your hearts and your minds in Christ Jesus.
Philippians 4: 6-7 NRSVCE

ROSALEEN McGUINNESS

HOLDING BACK

Lord You have asked us to "Come and See"
Then to "Go and tell"
But what holds us back
From accepting Your word
Is the knowledge of what we must sell

For we must let something go from our lives
That often our hearts hold dear
Still You continue to call us
Lord soften our hearts to hear

Perhaps we are like the 'rich young man'
Though You loved him, he could not stay
Lord give us the grace to hand over our lives

To Your will

Your work

Your way

Jesus, looking at him, loved him and said, "You lack one thing; go, sell what you own, and give the money to the poor, and you will have treasure in heaven; then come, follow me."
Mark 10: 21 NRSVCE

Rainbow

Lord of the Rainbow
Colour and shade
My heart's deep thanks
For the beauty You've made
A bridge to meet under
An arch to walk through
A fusion of colour
And all lead to You
Lord of the Rainbow
When doubt fills my mind
I look to the heavens
And know I will find
Your promise there painted
For each one to see
I wonder which colour
Best represents me?

Genesis 9:13

ROSALEEN MCGUINNESS, CO. ANTRIM, IRELAND

Rosaleen is a retired Health Care Professional and a practicing Catholic. She is also a professed Secular Franciscan and in the last six years has written eight 'Spiritual Reflection' publications, the narrative of which are based on her Franciscan spirituality. They reflect God's love as experienced in the wonder of creation and everyday life. She sincerely hopes that the narrative of her reflections will touch the lives of people and leave them with some sense of peace in a world of turbulence and change. Contact: bethanyhouse@talktalk.net

BRIAN MILLAR

Please Speak to Me

Sitting here in the deafened silence of the sun,

Explosions all around,

Riptide of gases raging by

In my eyes.

Atomic gestation over times

Is sending my head spinning

In billions of different directions,

Shooting out over years

Past earth and sky

And spinning planets.

I cannot hear you

Or the raging cosmos

In this star.

Please speak to me of Jesus,

Of meaning,

Of existence.

1 Kings 19: 12

BRIAN MILLAR

IN REALMS BEYOND

In realms beyond the thoughts of man
  God exists.

But his face is towards us,
  his love is upon us.

The exquisite beauty of his nature
  has woven together
  the genetic spirals
  of our existence.

(and his love is upon us)

His voice is like no voice
  that can be heard on earth,
  for in it are the springboards of creation,
  and all the codes of our universe
  from the elements to the eye of man.

And in the atom he has sung a song,
and microbe speaks to microbe
of the coming one,
and in His Book line on line
is revealed his plan.

In the beginning the Word already existed. The Word was with God, and the Word was God.

John 1: 1 NLT

BRIAN MILLAR

AND HE SHALL REIGN

The angels are singing
Over the throne of David,
Preparing it now for the coming One.

Soon the throne room
Will be built of stone
That cries out,
Jewels glowing with glory
In the entrance hall,
The very air
Imbued with light.

Revelation 7: 11

BRIAN MILLAR

To My Wife

I hold a baby's bottle in my hand
Feeding my child.
From cold hunger he came
When I met someone warm,
Who welcomed me
And grew to love me.
If love is the dream
Then marriage is the alarm clock,
And our love had to grow,
Had to grow, had to grow.
Expectations are not love,
Dreams are not love,
But you are, my love

Proverbs 18: 22

BRIAN MILLAR, LEIXLIP, CO. KILDARE
Born in Dublin, upon marriage to Marian in 1985, Brian migrated 10 miles to Leixlip. They now have two daughters, Esther and Ruth. He worked for 20 years as a postman, previously and presently self employed as a skilled handyman. Brian is currently developing a calling as a prophet and encourager. A member of the Christian Dance Fellowship of Ireland, and the Irish Christian Writers Fellowship, Brian moves and dances in worship, writes poetry and sometimes leads worship.
brianjmillar@yahoo.com

RUTH MILLAR

TRUE BEAUTY

Mirror, mirror on the wall,
Who is the fairest of them all?

You, my child, you are my all.
I created you.
I rescued you.
From this world and its works of perfection,
From this mirror and its lies of reflection,
From these hurts and those thoughts of rejection.

Mirror, mirror on the wall,
Who is the fairest of them all?

You, my child, you are my all.
Your beauty in me will never fall,
My love and strength will stand you tall.

My forgiveness is your cleanser,
My grace is your toner,
My word of truth is your make-up,
My presence is much bigger than a double D cup!

My breath is your life,
My presence is your beauty,
My hope within your eyes, cannot be contained
 within the confines of a looking glass.
But do not fret, do not give in,
 this fear of skin will pass.

Mirror, mirror on the wall,
Who is the fairest of them all?

It's me, of course!
Why do you ask?
My God, my King, His love is my mask.

Song of Solomon 2: 16

WORSHIP

My eyes feed off the sky with delight,
My soul it takes flight,
Heavenly Father, Your glorious might,
Yes, Amen! I stand for You in this fight.
Euphoria.
So light, ever bright, scented like a sweet pale essence of soft love,
Oh Father, my spirit flutters in delight,
Three in One, unite.

Epic, everlasting,
Euphoria.

(for my dad)

RUTH MILLAR, KNOCKNACARRA, GALWAY
"I am currently studying a fine art degree in Galway Mayo Institute of Technology. I began writing poems from the age of nine, when I first gave my life to the Lord. I was baptized in August 2013 and wrote a lot of poems around this time, I have always been creative minded and enjoy using words to express myself."

THE CALL

JONATHAN MULLEN

My voice and my ways are gentle, so be oh so quiet.
I stir in your heart and in your conscience,
I dawn on your soul in stillness,
I hide below, between and beyond your thoughts.
I am a word from a friend.
I whisper on the wind, through leaves and over the deep.
I am serendipity when you surrender.
I am in you and you in I.
When you are no more you will find me.

'And after the earthquake, fire, but the lord was not in the fire, and after the fire, a small still voice.

1 kings 19: 12

JONATHAN MULLEN, DUBLIN, IRELAND

Jonathan was born in 1969, a quiet child, crazy about fishing in his teens. In his early twenties, Jonathan studied illustration and loved it (he designed his own illustration above as well as the symbol illustrations in the margin of each page.) However in his twenties, Jonathan also developed schizophrenia and manic depression. When he was 32, he had an epiphany; he literally saw the light. For the first time he had a Faith. Now he is not just learning how to survive but, sometimes, thrive. He loves stillness and silence, and there he feels close to God.

Lamentations 3:22-26
(Because of the Lord's Great Love)

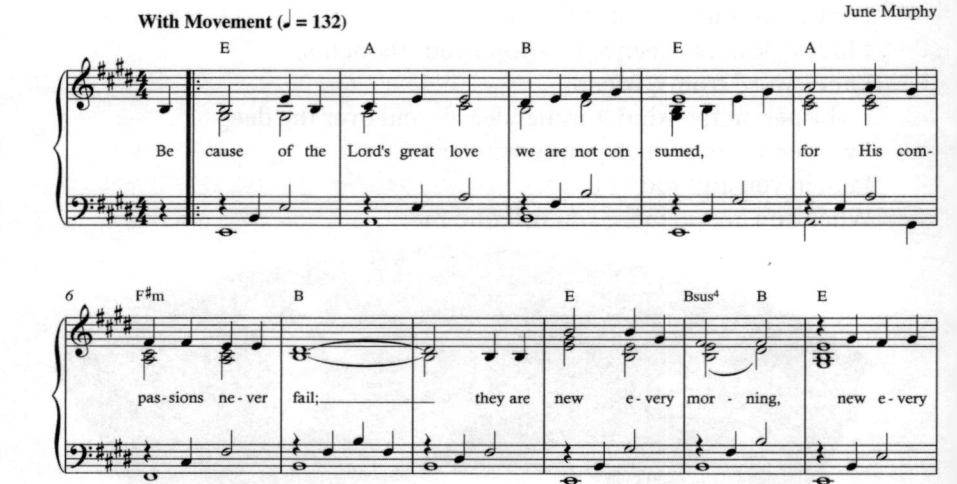

June Murphy

With Movement (♩ = 132)

Be - cause of the Lord's great love we are not con - sumed, for His com - pas - sions ne - ver fail; they are new e - very mor - ning, new e - very mor - ning; great is Your faith - ful - ness. I say to my - self the Lord is my por - tion, there - fore I will wait for Him.

Copyright © June Murphy 1995

Because of the Lord's Great Love (June Murphy)

Spiritual Songs, Poems and Prophecies

The Lord is good to those whose hope is in Him; to the One who seeks Him.

Be It is good to wait quietly for the Salvation of the Lord. It is good to wait quietly for the Salvation of the Lord.

Because of the Lord's Great Love (June Murphy)

The steadfast love of the Lord never ceases . . .
                                        Lamentations 3: 22-26 ESV

As the Deer

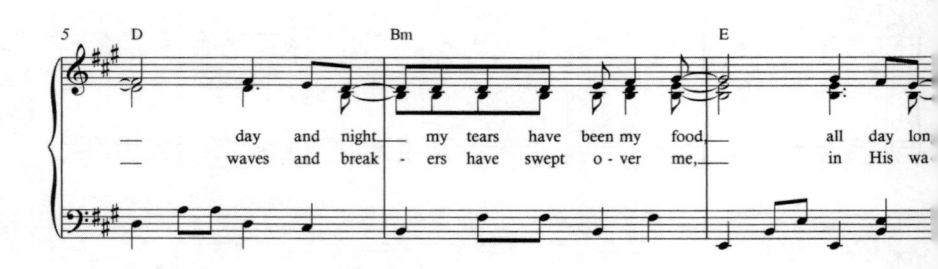

June Murphy

Moderate (♩ = 100)

1. As the deer pants for wa-ter, my soul longs for God;
2.,3. Where is God? My soul thirsts for the Li-ving God;

day and night my tears have been my food, all day long
waves and break-ers have swept o-ver me, in His wa-

I'm asked, "Where is your God?" Why are you so down-cast, O my soul
-ter-falls deep calls to deep.

so dis-turbed with-in me, O my soul? put your hope

Copyright © June Murphy 1999

As the Deer (June Murphy)

Spiritual Songs, Poems and Prophecies

...in God, for I will yet praise Him.
I will trust in God alone, my Salvation and my hope,
He's my mighty Rock, with singing lips I will praise Him as long as I live.
...Living God,
my soul thirsts for the Living God.

As the Deer (June Murphy)

*As the deer pants for the water brooks,
So my soul pants for You, O God.*

Psalm 42: 1 NKJ

JUNE MURPHY

NAMED

They thought
I'd arrive
on St. Patrick's Day
suiting
Patricia.

They said
had my birth been
at Christmas
their choice was
Noelle.

Instead
I arrived
late in March
so they christened me
June

Child of their Honeymoon.

Psalm 139: 13-16

JUNE MURPHY, CO. LONGFORD, IRELAND

"Born in Tullamore, Co. Offaly, I now live near Edgeworthstown, Co. Longford. Musician, songwriter, poet, wife, mother, and soon to be grandmother, my passion for song writing began as a teenager following an encounter with God. I enjoy playing the piano, singing new songs to the LORD, setting Scripture to music and composing new tunes for old hymns. There have also been seasons of writing poetry, with poems published in various anthologies, periodicals and local projects."

Lift Him Higher

I've searched throughout eternity
I've searched high and low
And Lord, I've found there's none like You in all the earth.

Unsearchable You—immortal, invincible.
No one compares to You, so faithful and so true.
You are the Lord, my Redeemer and Friend,
Splendor and majesty are before You.

Higher, higher, higher, higher
Exalt his holy name above
Higher, higher, higher, higher
Exalt His holy name on high.
Give Him praise, give Him praise,
Give Him praise.

For every mountain Lord, you've seen me through Lord.
I could not have done it, done it without You,
You're all powerful and ever loving,
Ever present in times of need.

Above all, holy One

Oh oh oh
I will bless the Lord.

Psalm 118: 28

REBECCA OLUWASEYI, DROGHEDA, IRELAND
Rebecca is an upcoming gospel artist based in Ireland with her family. An interior architecture and business student, Rebecca has a passion for singing and delivering God's word through the message of songs. She hopes to help and also touch lives with her gift.

INES BOUHANNANI

SONDER ANGEBOT : ALLES ZUM HALBEN PREIS

Regenmantel, bunt
wetterfest, enttaeuschungsresistent
zeitloser Schnitt , fuer sie und ihn

ZUM HALBEN PREIS

Himmelblaue Gebete , Hand gewebt
von hoeherer Stelle geprueft, federleicht ,
das ideale Geschenk fuer die Rastlosen

ZUM HALBEN PREIS

Gewuerzmischungen fuer alle Lebenslagen
 langzeit gestet, narrensicher,
fuer Spass mit Nebenwirkungen

ZUM HALBEN PREIS

DIESE SONDERANGEBOTE SIND NUR GUELTIG
fuer die Uebergangszeit
fuer die Schlaflosen, Mittelosen, Uebrig Gebliebenen

Es gibt keine Lieferzeiten
DIES IST ein EINMALIGES ANGEBOT
GREIFEN SIE ZU !

Markus 8: 36

Ines says, "I wrote this poem a while back, when I came to Ireland, and the Celtic Tiger was still roaring. There were offers everywhere, in all the supermarkets and shops. All the magazines were thick with pages of advertisement as well. I just wondered if this kind of effort could not also be done to promote other things, which we needs as well, but do not fit into a shopping bag."

INES BOUHANNANI

SPECIAL OFFER – BUY ONE GET ONE FREE

Multi-coloured raincoat
dream-washed, disappointment-proof,
A timeless fashion item/unisex.

BUY ONE GET ONE FREE

Azure blue prayers, hand-spun
Angel-approved, ultra-light
the ideal gift for desperation-suffers.

BUY ONE GET ONE FREE

A selection of spices to spice up your life
Clinically tested, fool-proof
for a great time with predictable side-effects.

BUY ONE GET ONE FREE

ALL OFFERS ARE ONLY VALID
for the time of transformation
for the sleepless, the hopeless and the penniless.

There are no participating SUPERMARKETS,
Please ask your local illusion-seller
for more information on these SPECIAL OFFERS
Mark 8: 36

INES BOUHANNANI, SHANNON, CO. CLARE
Ines was born in Frankfurt/Main, Germany, in 1968. In 1995, she moved to Hamburg to do a Masters degree in languages. Ines published poems in different literary magazines in Germany and won a number of writing competitions before moving to Ireland in 2003, where she began writing poetry in English. Ines has had some of her work published in "Stony Thursday" anthology /Limerick. Contact: inesbouhannani@yahoo.de

SEÁN Ó CEALLAIGH

SWEET SEASON WITH US STAY! AN ODE TO THE SEASON OF SPRING

Sweet Spring we welcome thee; how good to know
We now can part with frost and sleet and snow
We now to piercing cold can say "good-bye"
And welcome weather mild and sun-lit sky
May bid dark morns and afternoons adieu
And e'en at sunset nature's glories view.
How good again our favourite flowers to see
The fairy snowdrops peeping bashfully
The daffodils, while still in embryo
Shall surely soon in golden clusters glow
The pretty primsose'll visit us anew
And the bright bulbous crocus'll charm us too
Dear Lord we thank Thee that again we hear
Thy thrush and blackbird carol loud and clear
That we behold them now so blithe to be
To know that each of them is known to Thee!
What heavenly happiness to us they ring
As from the branch and bush and roof they sing
Fair Spring, may God thy session with us bless
Be to our sorrowing friends as joy no less
May they now know thy soothing influence too
To cheer and comfort them their sad lives through
We will not yet for summers blessings pray
But prize just thee; sweet season with us STAY!

Song of Solomon 2: 11-12

Seán Ó Ceallaigh

September Sadness

Should a new sadness on our bosoms weigh
E'en this September, seeing that summer's o'er
And those long days of sunshine are no more
And closer come with every fast-flying day
The darkness, cold, storms, sleet and snow showers, yeah
While as our barque draws nearer to the shore
Of Life's round sea, we wonder what's in store
For us when to this world farewell we pay.

Let's comfort take, when we reflect again
That we are fast approaching Christmas too
When our dear Saviour did born be
That He might die to save us – that we'll reign
If by His grace our faith we will renew
With Him in Heaven for all eternity!

Luke 18: 31-33

Seán Ó Ceallaigh

Christmas Day!

With glad hearts and voices
Let us praise and pray
While the world rejoices
On this Christmas day
When God's own Son has come awhile with us to stay.

Let's again the story
Joyfully recall
In cathedral hoary
In new gospel hall
How Jesus came on Earth to die and save us all

See Him helpless lying
On His makeshift bed
Hear Him softly crying
Wanting to be fed
Yes, He was born to die in torment in our stead

In the humble manger
In the stable bare
He is out of danger –
Let us have a care
To thank Him now that He has come our lives to share!

Jesus Lord we love Thee
Pardon us by grace
If we e'er did shove Thee
Into second place
Oh grant we'll serve Thee 'till we see Thee face to face

Spiritual Songs, Poems and Prophecies

And 'till then, let's ever
Help those us around
Let us vow to never
Wanting to be found
When any fellow-being by burdens sore is bound
Let us each day make it
Just like Christmas Day
Lets its spirit take it
Lets its message say
To everyone who hence across our paths may stray!

And suddenly there was with the angel a multitude of the heavenly host praising God and saying:
"Glory to God in the Highest,
And on earth peace, goodwill toward men!"
                                                                Luke 2: 13-14

Seán Ó Ceallaigh

The Christmas Crib – Revisited

I visited the Crib today
As I used to long ago
When a wee child I watched in awe
The baby Jesus lo!

When I would see Him helpless be
Upon His bed of hay
And hope He knew that I had come
With Him a while to stay.

That when He woke He'd see that I
Had come His friend to be
And that He'd raise His little head
And share a smile with me!

But when a life long later I
Came to the crib anew
'Twas not the baby Jesus Christ
Who pierced my poor heart through

No; 'twas the Saviour of the world
That in that Crib I saw
Who came to Earth us all to save
Us back to God to draw

For had He chosen not be born
On that first Christmas Day
He could not then have later died
To wipe our sins away

The only reason Christ was born
Was that He would die too
The perfect sacrifice become
To God for me and you.

And so the Crib I stand beside
Has meaning new for me
It is the door to Heaven fair
For all eternity!

Luke 2: 1-7

Seán Ó Ceallaigh, Dublin, Ireland

Dublin Solicitor Seán Ó Ceallaigh born in Bandon, has lived in Tramore, Midleton, Mallow and Kilkenny before marrying Pauline and seeing their nine children and nine grandchildren. Winner of 'Ireland's Own' Beginners short-story competition in 2009 and a regular contributor to 'The Candlestick', his publications comprise numerous articles, poems, tracts and two novels. He has other manuscripts awaiting publication. Seán's hobbies include cycling, gardening, golf, tennis, chess, reading, writing and thinking. His heroes and heroines include John Wesley, Cardinal Newman, Martin Luther King, Mary of Nazareth, Thérèse of Lisieux and Anne Frank. His dream is to meet all his friends in Heaven some day.

STEPHEN O'BRIEN

From God to the Children

I hear the cry of many a child
  Who is lonely lost and confused,
Because these precious little angels
  Were so hurted and abused.
Their little faces are so downcast
  And their hearts are broken too,
And still they blame it on themselves
  For something they failed to do.
And yet they put on a brave face
  And their smile can light up the sky,
Yet down deep in their hearts
  I can still hear them cry.
Yes they look at me with empty eyes
  And are afraid to call me 'Dad',
Forever in need of a loving hug
  It was nowhere to be had.
So they plod on down the road
  With their teardrops hitting the ground,
Looking for someone to love them.
  That someone will never be found.
Because I'm the One who loves you
  And I understand your fears,
I'll watch over and protect you
  And give you back your childhood years.

Joel 2: 25

STEPHEN O'BRIEN, DUBLIN, IRELAND
"I have lived all my life in or near Dublin City. The flats where I now live are being boarded up, one by one, to facilitate regeneration. I have lost three brothers to the effects of drugs, but I praise God and live in faith every day. And by God's grace, I am a teacher of the word of grace and faith, and I am seeing lives being transformed, including healings, through the ministry the Lord has given me, which equips the saints for ministry themselves. God is amazing."

DAMIEN O'NEILL

KEEP IT TRUE

Keep it true,
like a bow shoots an arrow.
Keep it true,
to the bone, to the marrow.
Keep it true,
at the loss of a friend.
Keep it true,
at the start, the middle, the end.
Keep it true,
amid the tales and the tattle.
Keep it true,
in the thick of the battle.
Keep it true,
in your heart, in your mind.
Keep it true,
and true treasure you'll find.

> . . . *whatever things are true, whatever things are noble, whatever things are just, whatever things are pure, . . . meditate on these things.*
>
> *Phil 4: 8*

DAMIEN O'NEILL, KILCOCK, CO. KILDARE
Damien was born 1965 Dublin.
He became a Christian in 1989 in Oxford, U.K.
Damien wrote his first poem in 1985.

GERARD O'SHEA

At Last . . . The Sea

Once in every life
Love steps in
We sometimes meet her at the door
And times we find within...
But whether that encounter
Lasts for all our days
Is all within our gift
As the Piper always pays

Whatever song we hum to
Is our soundtrack at the End
Whenever there's a turning
We cast aside a friend,
Until at last the Sea
O'erwhelms the rising flood
And all is sealed Conundrum...
Of true and pure and good?

Many waters cannot quench love

Song of Solomon 8:7 NLT

GERARD O'SHEA

AN APRIL DAY

There is a stillness here trapped by water
A place where time hangs suspended
Caught like a dragonfly in frozen elevation...
Pressed like a precious flower
Between the pages of a yellow book...
Every bush and tree and jumping fish
Performing to a symphony of calm,
And the ochroid furze on riverbank applauds
As the swan and water hen lithely skim
Their silent, graced ovation...
And every breath and bough that stirs
Cranes a neck to see the ebbing light
Of such a sweet and pleasant April day.

...the earth is full of his unfailing love.

Psalm 35:5 NLT

GERARD O'SHEA

MARKET FORCES

So many truths
Expressed in the check-out queue
Of seeking souls
Particles of meaning, high shelved
Out of the reach of the immature-
Two for one price packs of instant karma...
Soluble truth grains
Ideal for that mid-morning
Sense of nothing pick me up...
Yellow packed morsels of cake
For the bread demanding mob
More than empty heads
Will be lost in this revolution...
Mistress Truth still tantalises
Even in the black shadow
Of Madame guillotine.

All's not yet lost in this cost-cutting war
The truth has relatives
Long distanced, non-visiting
Like Real and Soul Integrity
Where the kindly guardian
May, even after closing time
Allow the briefest visit.

As for me I think I'll trust
In other than the Princes and their chariots,
And lie back as an infant child
Enjoying all the sustenance
Dropped at my feet
By kindly ravens.

*Ask and it **will** be given to you;*
*seek and **you will find**;*
*knock and the door **will** be opened to **you**.*

Matthew 7:7 NLT

GERARD O'SHEA

MOTHER

I was like a guide-dog
Leading my mother
Through the hazards of shopping centres
And crossing roads
As her eyes dimmed with age.

She bore it all bravely
And kept the tears
Till we were gone,
Then - in a flash of time
A light dawned
That spirited her away
From all our care and ken.

She had simply had enough.
And at the end
Sat back in her chair
And didn't even wave goodbye.

Now her eyes are wide open
And she is seeing things
We can only dream of.

And he said to this disciple, "Here is your mother."
John 19:27 NLT

GERARD O'SHEA, LIMERICK, IRELAND

Gerard O'Shea was born in Limerick in 1956. Writing poetry from the age of 10, his first published poem appeared in the school magazine and was a piece about the futility of war. In his late teens Gerard came to Christ and had a dramatic conversion experience that had a profound effect on his life and writing. Later he organised a monthly gathering for first time writers and out of this came an anthology, 'Dovetale'. His most admired poet is Emily Dickinson and takes her words, "This is my letter to the world, that never wrote to me" as his own maxim.

MARY OYEDIRAN

THE WIDOW IN OUR MIDST!

There she is again,
in our midst,
Always in red,
as if she is never fed!

Here she is again
in our midst;
she sticks out
like a traffic light
refusing to change from red!
Why can't she stay in bed!

Here she goes again,
stuck in our midst.
Smiling and cooing
like an old hen,
her feathers are bright red.
Who let her out of the pen?

Here she is again,
seating in our midst.
Doesn't she have a place to go?
Every day she's covered in red.
Where is she from, nobody knows!

She is here again
in our midst!
Standing! Clapping!
Why is she so happy!
Draped in that coat - Blood Red.

With all her woes and troubles,
she should have fled!

Here she is again
in our midst!
Jumping and singing,
swaying and dancing
with many other women
all dressed in pure, shocking red,
extremely happy and joyful despite
all the tears they shed!

Here they are again
in our midst!
Now I know who they are!
These are the Lord's widows!
Like me, their sins are forgiven.
Cleansed and washed by His Blood,
The blood of the Lamb of God!
They are set free! Yes! Free indeed!
To worship and adore their Saviour!
In His eyes, all widows find favour!

Here they are again
in our midst!
Our eyes have shunned them,
our mouth has taunted them,
our hearts have rejected them.
But You, Oh Lord, loved them!
Forgive us Lord,
Give us another chance.
Give us a new heart
so we can take a second glance.
With Your love abiding in us,
we promise to:
Reach out to all
Even when they fall!

Now you've read my poem, I have these questions:

> Have you prayed for a widow today?
> Have you phoned or text a widow today?
> Have you visited a widow today?
>
> Widows are precious to God!
> Are they precious to you?
> Why not adopt a widow and show her
> The Love of God!
> This is true religion!

Pure religion and undefiled before God is this, to visit the fatherless and widows in their afflictions and to keep himself unspotted from the world.

James 1:27 KJV

MARY OYEDIRAN, DUBLIN, IRELAND

Mary is a writer of short stories and poetry and a member of the Irish Writer Christian Fellowship. Recently widowed after 30 wonderful years, she has beautiful children and an adorable grandson. Surprisingly, the loss of her son and husband within 6 years had the most positive influence on her writing. The Holy Spirit revealed the purpose of Mary's writing through Proverb 31:8-9: her writing is a voice for the weak and defenceless. Mary says, "Ireland is great place for inspiration for Christian writers – there is so much to glean".

LEN PEARSON

WONDERFUL LOVE

So perfect His love,
So perfect His ministry,
He gave His life for me,
Then called out my name,
So perfect His love,
He gave me a brand new start
Mended a broken heart,
And set my soul free.

And the praise that I give
To Jesus my friend,
Is the joy of my heart,
Forever.

So perfect His love,
So perfect His love for me
That in the face of death
He still redeemed me
So perfect His love
Whose grace we now all can gain
Making us whole again
As He'd want us to be

For God so loved the world that He gave His only begotten Son, that whoever believes in Him should not perish but have everlasting life. For God did not send His Son into the world to condemn the world, but that the world through Him might be saved.
John 3: 16-17 NKJV

This is sung to the tune/music *'Wonderful Love'*

LEN PEARSON

THINK GREEN

As we glide thru the void
On this rock we call home
Trailing a dead moon in our wake.

As we travel thru space
Forever circling a sun
There is a decision to make.

As we ride thru the night
On this great orb of clay
The message is strident and clear.

As we pass by the stars
On this blighted sad rock
We are killing the home we love dear.

As we travel thru time
Shall we die, like the moon?
Or clean up our home and rejoice.

And journey still onwards
Seeing vistas anew
You know there is only one choice.

Genesis 1: 26-28

Len Pearson

I'M NOT SORRY

I'm not sorry that I turned to God,
For me it was no loss.
To turn away from wickedness,
And reach out for the Cross.

I'm not sorry that I sought the Lord,
For I saw that Holy Tree,
And now I know He died for us.
On that hill of Calvary.

I'm not sorry for the times I cried,
To my Saviour on that Tree.
In hope I reached to Jesus,
And He's surely set me free.

I'm not sorry that I called His name,
When I was feeling low,
He helped me find a place with Him,
Where love and goodness flow.

I'm not sorry for the choice I've made,
My life's been turned around,
For now I know my soul's been saved,
And I am Heaven bound.

For by grace you have been saved through faith, and that not of yourselves; it is the gift of God
Ephesians 2: 8

LEN PEARSON

EMBERS

When he came in from the night
He was given a light,
With joy I know he remembers,
But that lights now just a glow
It's dying down low
All that's left are a few glowing embers.

With the harsh words of a few,
Of the loved ones he knew,
Of his past they shouldn't remember,
They are killing the light,
It's no longer so bright
In the ashes there's only an ember

With his confidence shaken
Will his faith reawaken
Why must they always remember
Is his light doomed to die
To his Lord hear him cry
Please rekindle this guttering ember.

Yes He'll hold fast on to you
As an anchor that's true
For you know He'll never remember
With hope that His light
Will once more burn bright
Bursting forth from that flickering ember.

Hebrews 10: 23

LEN PEARSON

O, Tribune of Rome

O, Tribune of Rome,
With your sword and your spear,
Were you sorry you murdered my master?
Did you tremble with fear?
Did you not shed a tear
As you witnessed that day of disaster?

O, Tribune of Rome,
Did you heart feel a chill
When nailing my Lord to that cross?
But know if you will
My Lord, He lives still
For the Spirit of God set Him free.

O, Tribune of Rome
With your long bloody spear
Thrust so deep in the side of my master,
Did your conscience stay clear
As you thrust forth your spear
On the day that you murdered my master?

O, Tribune of Rome
Will you ever be free
From the guilt of killing my master?
Or did you like me
Go down on your knee
To be saved by the blood of our master?

Mark 15: 39

LEN PEARSON, CO. MAYO, IRELAND
Len came to the Lord late in life, having totally rejected the idea of a supreme being for forty years or more. He gave his heart to Jesus in 2000 and was baptised on Easter Sunday of that year. Len began writing poems to further his faith, expressing how he felt at the time. From poetry he branched out into full time writing. Two books are published and a third awaits a suitable ending. Len says, "God has blessed me greatly and I hope that he blesses you abundantly too."

SHAY PHELAN

SPARROWS

I'd rather be where my sparrows sing
Than hear the grand, majestic strains
Of proud symphonies.

My sparrows are only small,
Their feathers are only brown and untidy.
I dress my sparrows in light of sun,
My poor ones shine translucent
In the beauty and the glory of my Word.
They feed from my hands my choicest crumbs,
And spread their tiny wings to fly
As high as they can! –
So small! –
They never fly too far from my hands.

The chirping and the chattering and the joy of the fledglings
Rejoice my heart in the midst of the darkness,
In the squalor of the sin-torn streets, my little ones need me –
Yes, and it moves my heart to see how they need me –
And my joy is in the meeting of their needs.

I'd rather be where my sparrows sing
Than hear the grand, majestic strains
Of proud symphonies.

1 Peter 5:6-7

"Both 'Sparrows' and 'The Treasure in the Earthen Vessel' were written during a time when I was fellowshipping with Christians who were living in a tough part of Dublin, where there were some big social problems, including drug addiction. Some friends had been affected by such issues, but it was so tantalisingly beautiful to see the love of God flowing in their lives, even in their struggles, and to hear their voices raised in praise and love of Him. You could not have paid me to miss the meetings there."

SHAY PHELAN

The Treasure in the Earthen Vessel

Like moonlight on an old slate roof
Or lamplight in a pool of rain;
The frost that gleams on lean, black branches,
The starlight over dark terrain;
    The smile of joy upon a face
    Long lined with cares, now kissed by grace –
The treasure in the earthen vessel,
Oh how sweet that is to see...

The thief who once stole everything
Now working with his hands to give,
The gift he gives is very small
But oh, how strangely beautiful;
    A ray of sun in old, dark rooms,
    Lazarus staggering from his tomb –
The treasure in the earthen vessel,
Oh, how sweet that is to see!

And we are all like delicate leaves
Fading in these autumn days;
And yet we form a precious glove
Upon the outstretched hand of love.
    The body broken on the cross –
    Love's triumph in love's seeming loss –
The treasure in the earthen vessel,
Oh how sweet that is to see.

2 Corinthians 4:6-7

SHAY PHELAN

LORD OF AGAPE

Love, there is nothing but love, radiant and child-like,
    pure and innocent light,
Glimmering and shimmering more than all the stars in the night.
I'm living in Love, giving in Love, dreaming in Love;
    I'm resting in Love's eternal embrace;
I'm yearning and yearning in Love to seek Love's face.

Love made me, pre-planned me, created me;
    Love mourned for me when I was lost – Love saved me;
When I despised and crucified Love, Love died for me and rose again
– Love reclaimed me.
I'm lifted in Love, gifted in Love,
    seated in Love's high places in Love's eternal domain;
I'm hidden in Love but I shall appear with love
    when He comes in glory again.
    Chorus: Oh Lord of Agape, so pure, so true;
        Oh Lord of Agape, joins me to you –
        He's so pure and strong and true.

Love so majestic yet so intimate,
    Love so stern sometimes – Love so beautiful;
Love working in the groaning hearts of men life incorruptible.
Love so mysterious and strange,
    burning like fire, blazing like a mighty flame;
Love causing the blind to see and healing the lame.
    Chorus: Oh Lord of Agape, so pure, so true;
        Oh Lord of Agape, joins me to you –
        He's so pure and strong and true.

Love, there is nothing but love, radiant and child-like, pure and innocent light,
Glimmering and shimmering more than all the stars in the night.

1 John 4: 16

SHAY PHELAN

The Sword that Slays the Enemy

Oh the shadows of your former lives,
They trouble you sometimes.
They whisper in your listening ears
And prey upon your mind.
They tell you that you're still a slave,
They say you have to fall!
But the shadows of your former lives
Are liars, one and all.

Oh the shadows of your former lives
Are whispering to you yet.
They tell you that you're still a slave
To the law of sin and death.
They hold you in your prison cell,
Though the door is open wide –
And they keep you from the victory
For which our Saviour died.

Come out, come out, like Lazarus,
From this tomb of doubt and fear!
Let us cast aside the grave clothes
We need no longer wear.

For the word of God speaks living truth
That we, to these shadows, are dead.
I look, I see not what you were,
I see Christ instead.
He's radiant in His victory
And we in Him are one –
I look, I see not what you were,
In Christ we are reborn.

And why should memory waken fear
If ever I recall
The thing I was, or anything you did,
For Jesus bore it all.
He bore my sin to death with Him
And all its power is lost!
The thing I was, or anything you did
Has perished on the cross.

And we can walk in victory
Don't listen to the devil's lies!
For the power that resurrected Christ
Now lives in you and I.
And the sword that slays the enemy
Is waiting in our hands!
Why do we stand in the Promised Land
With our heads still buried in the sand?
Why should we stand in the Promised Land
With our heads still buried in the sand?

Therefore, there is now no condemnation for those who are in Christ Jesus, because through Christ Jesus the law of the Spirit who gives life has set you free from the law of sin and death.
Romans 8:1-2 NIV

"The enemy is, of course, spiritual and not carnal, and our sword is the Word of God. This song celebrates the victory that is ours in Christ as we learn to take hold of all that the Word tells us about who we are in Him – and all that He is in us."

Shay Phelan

More Beautiful the Face of Jesus

More beautiful the face of Jesus
Than precious works of art,
For in the lovely face of Jesus
We'll see His loving heart.
      No false expression there to hide
      His pure and innocent light.

And more wonderful the word of Jesus
Than the poets' greatest lines;
For in the wond'rous word of Jesus
We'll see His awesome mind.
      No promise there we can't believe,
      No lies to harm or grieve.

Jesus, Jesus, your truth endures forever;
Jesus, Jesus, your word will fail me never.

And more glorious the love of Jesus
Than even the brightest dawn.
Though daylight turn to night time,
Your love burns ever on.
      No shadow there to dim the flame,
      Your love burns ever the same.

      Jesus, Jesus, your love endures forever;
      Jesus, Jesus, your love will fail me never.

More beautiful the face of Jesus.

2 Corinthians 4:6

Shay Phelan, Dublin, Ireland
A native of Dublin and long-time member of St Mark's Church, Shay, in his younger days, worked in theatre, gaining valuable acting experience. More recently, he has developed a ministry involving dramatic presentations of scripture and short dramas expressing the Christian message, performed in church events, services and conferences. Shay also performs story-telling sessions for children. He can be contacted at: shaypphelan@gmail.com

SARAH-JAYNE POMEROY

'THE LAND OF MILK AND HONEY'
a poem about finding true faith outside the walls of religion

I have been to the land of milk and honey,
A place beyond compare.
The grass is good, the water is fine,
I'd like to take you there.

But you still graze in the lands of Egypt,
Thinking that your stubble is hay.
Enslaved into a system of death,
Believing Egypt is the only way.

Could I tell you what I've seen?
Would you even want to know?
Would you accept the freedom available?
Would you really want to go?

In my heart I have so much to tell,
Of the freedom I have seen,
I have tasted the living water,
And grazed on grass so green.

Egypt is the place in our minds,
The place of disbelief,
The idea that things never really change,
There is never any relief.

Jesus died to change our lives,
To save us all from death,
To give us joy and peace everlasting,
To fill us with His breath.

Of these things we all know,
Of these things we all speak,
But where is the evidence in our hearts,
Despite our knowledge, our words are bleak.

Love, peace, joy and faith,
Are words that should be tangibly felt,
More than just a mantra we speak,
More than pieces of theology dealt.

To Jeremiah did he say,
"My Law on their hearts I will write..."
Those words that were on stone and pages
Are no longer words that we just recite.

The hypocrisy of our religion,
It leaves me in despair,
I want to see love in action,
Believers that truly care!

Testimonies of white-washed tombs,
Churches full of bones,
WE are now the living dead!
And how the Spirit groans.

The cheap counterfeit 'so great',
Is this what we accept?
Do we know of nothing more
Than this doctrine that inward crept?

But I've been to the land of milk and honey,
A place beyond compare.
The grass is good, the water is fine,
I'd like to take you there.

Ephesians 5: 8, 14

SARAH-JAYNE POMEROY

'GOODBYE BELFAST'

To Belfast, which was once of kings,
 of storytellers, music player, and beautiful queens.
Over the years the songs changed,
 and the music did fade.
The kings and queens died,
 and plunged the country into shade.

Your people cried out in despair,
 their heads hung low in shame.
Your tribes, wrought in battle,
 wrapped your country in pain.
They fought for a freedom,
 but to it, became their slaves.
Lo, darkness and depression,
 it flooded in like waves.

But Goodbye Belfast,
 this will be you no more.
Arise a country of saints and scholars,
 which the world will stand to adore.
The throne which lies empty,
 will no longer be void.
HIS praises from her hills,
 you will sing them out loud.

HE will truly set out,
 and set your captives free.
Blind eyes will open,
 opened for all to see.
To those who cried out in Belfast,
 you will now cry out in joy.

For the Kingdom has come!
His kingdom is here now.

But Goodbye Belfast,
for now my time has come,
To leave this dear city,
to follow after the son.
As the birds fly in winter,
so I'm headed south.
"Go build my Kingdom"
He told me from His mouth.

So Goodbye Belfast I pray,
  Become all you are called to be,
A city of kings, story tellers, music players,
  A city of the free.

> *The voice of one crying in the wilderness: "Prepare the way of the LORD; . . . The glory of the LORD shall be revealed, and all flesh shall see it together; for the mouth of the LORD has spoken."*
> *Isaiah 40:3-5* NKJV

SARAH-JAYNE POMEROY, CO.LEITRIM, IRELAND
Sarah-Jayne is a Christian author, blogger and missionary with a heart for truth. In 2014 she founded The Noah Mission, a family missions project which is currently building a boat to sail 12000 miles from Ireland to the Philippines! Originally from Belfast, she currently resides in County Leitrim where she and her husband jointly run a smallholding called 'The Wilderness Farm', while home schooling their five young children.

KENNY RASAKI

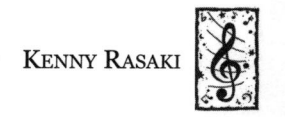

BLESS YOU LORD

I bless You
I bless You
Oh, oh, Lord,
I bless You
I bless Your holy name

I bless You
I bless You
Oh, oh, Lord,
I bless You
I bless Your holy name

I bless Your name
I bless You, oh, oh, Lord,
I magnify You, I worship You . . .
Your name – holy name.

Repeat chorus: I bless You . . . *till fade*

> *'I will bless the Lord at all times;*
> *His praise shall continually be in my mouth.*
>
> *Psalm 34: 1 NKJV*

KENNY RASAKI

JESUS, HALLOWETH BE YOUR NAME

Je----sus, halloweth be your name
Je----sus, halloweth be your name

4xe

Halloweth be Your name oh Lord   *(lead)*
Halloweth be Your name   *(response)*
4xe

Honour to your name oh lord   *(lead)*
Halloweth be your name   *(response)*

Matthew 6: 9

KENNY RASAKI, ATHLONE, IRELAND
Kenny's full name is Kehinde Rasaki. Born and educated in Nigeria, Kenny is married with two lovely girls. She is Praise and Worship Leader in her local church. Kenny's mission is to reach the lost, sharing with them the massage of God's saving love through music and songs. Her focus is to exalt and magnify the name of Jesus Christ.

MARK DAVY

JESUS

I was walking down the street
I met a guy called JESUS
I was gonna get *drunk*
I was gonna get *stoned*
My heart was breaking
I felt all alone

Jesus reached out His hand
Lifted me out of all my strife
Gave me A PURPOSE
Gave me A PROMISE of eternal life

He said I'M CALLING YOU, MARK
I've got a really good plan
There's a hurting world out there
-*Dying* – waiting for a helping hand
I'm sending you to show my love
Dare to show how much I care
Go to the Nations and throughout all lands
Tell them I love them JUST AS THEY ARE!

> 'Go into all the world and preach the gospel to every creature. He who believes and is baptised will be saved . . . '
> *Mark 16: 15 NKJV*

MARK DAVY, SOUTH YORKSHIRE, ENGLAND

Mark has a calling on his life to be a rap artist for the Lord, travelling to different nations, getting the message out to young people that Jesus loves them and has a special place for each of them in God's family. Mark's Nana, who Mark loved very much, came from County Donegal, Ireland. Mark was baptised in the sea in County Cork.

JOHN PURCELL

The Robin

The reason the robin has a red breast
Is it picked the thorns from God's head –
The blood poured on to its chest

The robin sings at Christmas each year
To bring us good cheer

The robin was my mother's best friend
When it sang its song it made her happy
Right to the end

So thank God for the robin
Who has brought us great joy
I have loved him ever since I was a boy

Matthew 10: 29

JOHN PURCELL, KILKENNY, IRELAND
John, one of seven children, remained home as an adult to care for his mother. Together they loved God's gift of creation, especially the robin. John loves to sing and has a powerful voice. He is heralded as the 'Kilkenny Cats' hurling team's most faithful supporter.

PHILIP ROBINSON

STILL FAITH IS

The ultimate freedom,
The fuel of hope,
An illogical passion.
The search for one truth
Leads to infinite questions,
Innumerable evidence,
A sandstorm of axioms.
There is always one 'x'
That remains unknown;
The Universal expansion:
New unturned stones.
Rest from your turning,
Breathe, look above,
Choose to believe,
Have faith,
Live
Love.

Jude 1: 20

PHILIP ROBINSON

FATHER, YOU ARE SIGHT

Father, You are sight beyond the blur of reason;
Father, You are light, we grow within your seasons.
Failure is our word that You despise with Love -
Father, You are sight beyond the sky above.

Father, You are sight, revealing new Your splendour;
Father, may Your will our hearts' endeavour.
Leaving comfort's home to face the ocean's span -
Father, You are sight beyond tomorrow's plan.

Father, You are sight, assurance in the darkness;
Father, You are truth, Tho' unknown is the abyss.
Chances we thought lost become a treasure found -
Father, You are sight, out guide when underground.

Father, You are sight, restoring blinded vision;
Father, You define the wisdom of all wisdom.
Worth and standards change each day but You remain!
Father, You are sight, we praise Your changeless Name!

Inasmuch as there is none like You, O LORD
(You are great, and Your name is great in might)
JEREMIAH 10: 6 NKJV

PHILIP ROBINSON

REASONABLE NEWS

Becoming older,
Draped in experience,
Equipped to be wiser:
Separation, sickness and death
Shadow our expectancy.
Every out-of-town phone call,
Email labelled "News",
Long-lost contact appearing
Now "recently viewed",
Calibrate our emotions
For a pending occasion -
Hope will be challenged,
Souls led to abandon
The faith our spirits
Consume for survival.
When prayers seem selfish,
Foolish and childish,
Miraculous acceptance
Replaces our wishes;
Love reminds us:
Life is more precious
Than all we try
To hold on to.

Psalm 16: 11

PHILIP ROBINSON, BELFAST, NORTHERN IRELAND
Originally from Barbados, Philip is an IT Consultant by profession, a Christian by confession and a poet & musician by passion. Philip started to play piano and compose for worship in his early teens, becoming a singer, songwriter and arranger for the Ask God Acappella group, releasing the album "All for Christ" in 1998. He recently released an EP entitled "More than DNA", declaring freedom from our past through love found in Christ. He is involved in the worship ministry of the Christian Fellowship Centre (CFC), Belfast. He and his wife Nicole's 2 children were both born in Belfast.

PAULINE SEXTON

TEACH ME TO LOVE

I search for love and as I do
I never think to look for you
Lord I know your Word is true
In everything I say and do
Teach me how to love I pray
There is a more excellent way!

Your Word is Light unto my feet
I love to hear your words so sweet
Love, the greatest thing of all
Is there for me each time I fall
And by my side I know you'll stay
There is a more excellent way!

I need to know that love is true
Yet real true love is found in you
Teach me how to walk in love
With words and deeds that rise above
The hollow words and games we play
There is a more excellent way!

... And now I will show you the most excellent way
1 Cor. 12:31

PAULINE SEXTON

AT HIS THRONE

I took you to His throne today
I laid you at His feet
I know that He will comfort you
And all your needs He'll meet

I took you to His throne today
I carried you in prayer
I told Him all about your needs
And then I left you there

I wanted to hold onto you
And care in my own way
But when I laid you at His throne
He said "Now walk away"

And so I left you at His throne
Surrounded by His love
Your needs are there before Him
In His throne room up above

> *Let us therefore come boldly to the throne of grace, that we may obtain mercy and find grace to help in time of need.*
> *Heb 4:16 NKJV*

PAULINE SEXTON

THE DAY OF VICTORY IS COMING

Don't lose heart in times of trouble
When despair comes rushing in
For even in the darkest days
He sees the victory you will win

When we are in the midst of trouble
And all we see is pain and fear
Jesus sees the day of victory
And He knows it will appear

In the darkest of situations
When every shred of hope is gone
Jesus is our strength and comfort
For in the darkness He sees the dawn

The day of victory is coming
Just let Jesus be your friend
He is the Alpha and Omega
He sees the beginning and the end

Isaiah 46:10, Ps 139

PJ SEXTON

ETERNITY

As time passes by do you look to the sky?
To the home that could be yours some day
Or do you spend all your time in the here and now
As if you were here to stay?
I'll tear down my barns and make them higher
There's so much that I have to do
But tonight as you sleep
The good Lord He could speak
"Your soul is demanded of you"
I'm not ready to die, this must be a lie
For now I will burn in the fire!
Because I lived for myself and the things of this world
Were always my heart's desire
I am the way, the truth and the life
Eternal life is in me
So don't get caught up in the trappings of time
But open your eyes and see
That beyond this world with its worries and cares
There's a much greater life to come
And the only way there is to draw near to God
And give your life to Jesus His son

Luke 12:16-22

PJ Sexton

The Potter and the Clay

Oh God I will worship. Oh God I will praise
Strength and power you give to my days
Glory and honour your grace and your love
All of your beauty that comes from above

Mould me and make me to whatever you may
You are the potter and I am but clay
Gently touch me with your skilled hand
A vessel of honour, here I stand

Yield to the potter, give Him your day
Allow Him to touch you, like hands upon clay
Changed to the image of His only Son
The work of the potter someday will be done

So come to the potter and seek His heart
For you are His vessel, He's set you apart
Then you will worship and humbly say
"You are the potter and I am but clay"

But now, O LORD, You are our Father;
We are the clay and You are our potter;
And all we are the work of Your hands.

Isaiah 64:8

PJ Sexton

Just As

Just as the stars come out at night
My promise holds no need to fight!

Just as night follows day
My promise holds have faith to pray

Just as clouds bring on the rain
My promise holds in all your pain

Just as salmon begin to spawn
My promise holds when hope is gone

Just as fruit falls from the tree
My promise holds, just wait and see

Just as the tides go in and out
My promise holds no need to doubt

Just as autumn leaves will die
My promise holds I cannot lie

Just as death leads into life
My promise holds now end your strife!

Where is the wise? Where is the scribe? Where is the disputer of this age? Has not God made foolish the wisdom of this world?
1 Cor 1:20 NKJV

PAULINE SEXTON

Time for Jesus

When the end has come
And there's nowhere to run
When you try to cope
But there's just no hope
When the pain inside just won't subside
And your heart is filled with deep despair
That's the time. That's the time
The most important time of all
That's the time . That's the time
For Jesus He will hear your call

When everything just falls apart
And you have no hope within your heart
When the burden's heavy on your back
And you're waiting for the next attack!
With questions spinning round and round
And not one answer can be found
And you call for help but no one is there
That's the time. That's the time
The most important time of all
That's the time . That's the time
For Jesus He will hear your call

Psalm 46:1-3 NKJV

PAULINE SEXTON

Number Nine

To all the children God
blessed her with, my Mother
gave as she was fit
Always mixing up the names,
    she went through eight before mine came!

I always thought that number one, must have had all the fun
Where she went we all would follow, I know my reasoning was hollow.

I would have settled for two or three, a place of importance in our
family
Four or five was quite okay, no real reason to complain.

Six or seven? Well not the best. But still as important as the rest
Even eight you could say was quite important in its own way.

But number nine! Oh Lord I wait for an explanation for my sorry fate!
Always last and always small, always youngest, no hope at all!

Last place I would always take, always blamed for their mistakes
Peggy toddles I was called left to toddle behind them all

Swung around and lifted high, from one to another made to fly
No matter how old I would grow, I would always be the baby you
know!

And so I ask You Lord explain just why, you chose me for this pain
Your answer is so simple just, You know the last shall be the first!

And as I sit and think it through, I know that yes, Your Word is true
I'm number nine you chose that way, but first in Your heart
I'll always stay

PJ Sexton

Love Is the Answer

Chorus
Love is the answer, love is the key
Love breaks down the barriers between you and me
Love keeps no record of all that is wrong
Love from the Father is pure and it's strong

A new commandment I give you today
Love one another for love leads the way
Love the Lord your God with all your heart, soul and mind
Don't forget your neighbour, don't leave him behind

This new commandment I give you today
It's not written on stone or on tables of clay
It's the love of Jesus that's shining in your heart
Given by the Spirit, it sets you apart

This new commandment I give you today
Was bought by the saviour, the price He did pay
It comes from the Father who lives up above
He gave us His Spirit to teach us His love

> 'A new commandment I give to you, that you love one another; as I have loved you, that you also love one another.'
> *John 13:34*

PJ Sexton

Cords of Human Kindness

With cords of human kindness I will lead you
I'll pick you up like an infant to my cheek
Bending down I will always feed you
My pleasure is in the lowly and the meek

It was I who taught you how to walk
I was there when you began to talk
You didn't know that it was I who healed you
I am always there no matter what you do

You always turned away and broke my heart
My son you were rebellious from the start
I will never give you up because of love
And home to me you'll fly just like a dove

Hosea 11

PJ & Pauline Sexton, County Cavin, Ireland

"We are a married couple who enjoy writing poetry, which we believe is inspired by the Holy Spirit. Our poems are based on the Bible and we see each one as a gift from God for our edification. Many of our poems have helped us through the storms of life or have brought scripture to life for us. They are also a gift to be shared with others and so we consider it a great privilege and pleasure to share them." Contact: paulinesexton@hotmail.com

ROGER SKILLINGTON

GENEROSITY TOWARDS GOD

Now is the time to give to the Lord
The life He has given to you,
To surrender to Him all that you are,
All that you want or have.
This is the time to surrender your will,
To make His will your own.
For the Lord is requiring a people,
Who are wholly committed to Him,
Who will go where He wants them to go,
And do what He wants them to do,
And to constantly know His will,
To hear His voice ever,
To say no to Him never,
But to be always His willing slave,
To surrender to Him in thought and in deed,
To surrender to Him all that you need,
For He will provide for His children,
And nothing will be lacking for them,
For only in doing His will completely
Will you find happiness and peace.

Commit your way to the Lord,
Trust also in Him,
And He shall bring it to pass

Psalm 37: 7

ROGER SKILLINGTON

ADORATION

I worship You oh Lord my God,
My King, my Jesus, my Saviour,
My one true Love, my deepest Hope,
My Joy, my Peace eternal.
Your praise is ever on my lips.
Your presence is all I need.
So take me deeper into You,
That I may die and You may live
    through me.
How much I love You, oh my Lord,
I can't find words to sa-ay.
I give You all my life my Lord
To use in Your own way.
A living sacrifice I bring,
To You, my Jesus, my Saviour.
May all my deeds bring joy to You,
My King, my Lord, my God.

Revelation 5: 8-9

ROGER SKILLINGTON

Our God Is

From eternity before,
To eternity evermore,
Our God Is. Is. Is.
He created all we see.
He created you and me.
And He speaks to us right now,
    (Can't you hear?)
"I love you. I love you. I love you."
    Chorus:
Let us dance and sing.
Let us praise our King.
And give our God the Glory.   (X2)

To us He is so-o dear,
For His presence is always near.
Our God Is. Is. Is.
He is precious in our sight.
He dwelleth in eternal light
Yet He reaches down to say,
    (Can't you hear?)
"I love you. I love you. I love you."

Chorus:
Won't you come to this God now?
He is longing to show you how.
He who Is. Is. Is.
He will open you a flood.
He will cleanse you in His blood.
He will speak to you and say,
    (You will hear.)
"I love you. I love you. I love you."

Exodus 33: 14

ROGER SKILLINGTON

CHRISTIAN RAP

My life was a mess, as I walked the broad way,
So I called out to Jesus and He came in to stay.
He opened my heart and he came inside.
He said. "Son relax, I'm taking over this ride.
I'm gonna drive the car of your life from now on.
You will be safe in my hands my son."
So I turned my life around to His way,
Now I feel so happy that all I can say
Is. "Thank You Lord for all you've done.
Thank You for calling me your son."
   Now if you're feeling down and out,
And there's nothing you can do about
The hurt and pain that you are feeling,
Or the sorrow deep within you reeling,
Just turn to God and put your trust
 In the name of Jesus—man that's a must—
You'll feel so happy and full of joy,
Just like a boy who's just received a brand new toy,
But it's not a toy that you'll have got
But Jesus Christ the Son of God.

Psalm 91: 1

ROGER SKILLINGTON, CORK, IRELAND

Born in 1940 into a very religious family, I always had a faith and a fear of God and attended services all the time. In 1977 I received 2 books from my sister in America "Shout it from the Housetops" and "They Speak in tongues", both telling of people's interaction with the God of creation. Very shortly after that I invited Jesus into my life and was completely changed internally. Since then the Lord has been giving me poetry and I have collected them on my computer. spear22man@yahoo.co.uk

HARRY SMITH

HE WALKS THE LAND . . .

In Ireland, and here also,
    I step on to your land.
A land, and hearts scarred ...
    as you were moved, coerced, forced towards the setting sun.
Like a great earth-mover we pushed, pushed, pushed you before us ...
    ripping, tearing at your very roots.
The blood cries out!

I sit among you listening.
In some strange, profound way,
    I feel your pain, His pain.
At times gentle, quiet,
    at others ...
        gut wrenching, agonizing – PAIN!

In their thousands they came
    - my people, my tribe,
        to fulfil their destiny,
            yet destroying yours.
They knew not, that God had also put "eternity in your hearts".
They knew not, that He wanted to redeem you and your culture too
    – another way!
"Father forgive them" – did they truly know not what they did?

"During the days of His life on earth, He offered up prayers, petitions,
    with loud cries and tears ... and He was heard."
He still does ...
    walking your land, my land, still crying, weeping, still heard -
        through those He finds, to share it with ...
            to stand among you, and weep.
There is still a destiny, a dignity for you.
Still available, now being restored – IN HIM!

Hebrews 5: 7

HARRY SMITH

LISTEN!

It stands alone in a tree shaded place,
beside a church in Harbor Springs.
A white, wreathed, Indian feathered, cross.
I stand there and listen.
Listening to a cry, not only in the heart of God
but also to another, rising up from the ground.

For over one hundred and fifty years,
on a nearby plot of land,
ever enlarging walls engulfed the lives of Native young -
The Holy Childhood of Jesus Residential School -
thousands in an unholy embrace.

Listen!
As they were torn from their homes,
transported,
debraided,
language and culture supressed.
Many died, to be placed in unmarked graves!
Others, still alive,
are left still dying,
in so many different ways
- on the inside!

Listen!
Creator's Son, with arms stretched out,
embraces the wounds of history.
His blood also cries out, better than that of Abel.

The Father hears ...
and ...
folding you in His arms,
He releases redemption, healing, forgiveness, dignity, hope!

Be still! Listen!
Can you hear the Blood,
His heart - for you?

Harry shares: Like *'He Walks the Land'*, the poem, *'Listen'*, was born out of a ministry trip. In 2013 we visited Harbor Springs in northern Michigan, where I was confronted with the issue of Residential Boarding Schools for Native American children. There had been a school there, run by the Catholic Sisters of Notre Dame (1829 -1983). It was part of a misguided social experiment of assimilation, initiated by the State and overseen by a number of different Churches, in which tens of thousands of Indian children, were removed from their families, to experience the humiliation of having their braided hair cut and being punished for speaking their Native language. Many, susceptible to communicable diseases, died in these schools and were placed in unmarked graves.

"The school is no longer there, having been replaced by a modern Parish building. All we saw, in a shaded area close to the nearby Church, was a simple white Cross with Native feathers hanging on it. As I stood there before it, weeping rose up from within my spirit, which later prompted the writing of this poem. I was very conscious that a deep wound within the Native American people regarding the legacy of these Boarding Schools still needs to be healed.

"A few days later I read these scriptures: **'Listen!** *Your brothers blood cries out from the Ground'* (Genesis 4:10), in which God speaks to Cain about the murder of his bother Abel, and Exodus 3:7&9, *'I have indeed seen the misery of my people ... I have heard them crying out ... I am concerned about their suffering ... the cry of the Israelites has reached me ...'* Nothing goes unnoticed by our God!"

HARRY SMITH, BELFAST, NORTHERN IRELAND

"Having spent 18 years in a residential community for prayer and reconciliation in Ireland, I am now in a season of transition, where the embracing of the ancient wounds in Ireland between Catholics and Protestants has been the catalyst in a most unexpected encounter with another culture - equally wounded by my English/Scotch-Irish forefathers - the Native Americans in the USA. I have found that in our complex histories both sides have been the losers; the wounded wound! And yet, there is hope as God, through our reconciler Jesus Christ, seeks to use us as His channels to bring healing to all. My poems are a reflection of that." www.dignityrestored.org

BRENDA VANWINKLE

THE SOUND, THE SCENT OF GREEN

Blades of grass
Ferns
Moss
Leaves
A cacophony of green sound.

The rustle of life
The dance of green.

Blue seas clap rocky shore
The sound of green.

Artist's palette of innumerable hues
Painting that which no
earthly artist
has yet
dreamed.

Layers of living,
vibrating,
movement
as Breath
of
God
breathes.

Each vista captures and
displays the
Sound, the Scent
of green.

Ps.92:12-15

BRENDA VANWINKLE

TURNING

Fatherless wanderers
Looking for home
Motherless victims
Destined to roam
Over the oceans, facing the deep
Searching in nations
A place for safe sleep.

Look in a bottle
Trust in that which cannot feed
Ache in my belly
Soul ravished with need.
Anger against me
The slap of a hand
Violence my stronghold
I run to withstand.

Hidden deep within lies a seed dormant long
A whisper, a remembrance of
Forgotten song
Ache. Longing. Desiring for more
Voice stilled, expression shunned
Freedom a closed door.

Then out of the darkness
A rumbling, a sound
Emanates from long ago
Prayers that saturated air and ground.
A cadence, a drumbeat,
The call of the pipe
Ancient tones of high praises
Break through the night.

Beat of a Father's heart
Redefining son's identity
Inheritance reserved for daughters
Coming home from across the sea.

Orphans no longer!
A nation receives her voice
Belonging, Believing, Becoming
As high heaven and
Deep earth rejoice.

The Spirit you received does not make you slaves, so that you live in fear again; rather, the Spirit you received brought about your adoption to sonship. And by him we cry, "Abba, Father." The Spirit himself testifies with our spirit that we are God's children.
Rom. 8:15-16 NIV

BRENDA VANWINKLE

OPEN

Uncertain of which key
fits which lock,
I wait.

Listening. Postured to hear,
My one certainty is
that there are locks
to which I
hold
the
key.

Energy and resources
Designed to be activated once inside
grant an awareness that
I must
Not consume them with self-effort of seeking
which door?
which lock?

But wait.
Rest.
To hear.   To know.
Eyes open.   Ears alert…

Then I hear!

Stillness invaded by a sure
Vibration,

The cry of those held captive
escapes through
long overlooked

keyholes
and I hear.
I feel.
I know.
I go.

Keys fashioned by centuries of
DNA arching
toward destiny,
tempered by faithfulness
in years of trial.

Fire has formed patterns in
my deep places
and I see.
I realize.   I know.

I am the key, held in a firm and sure grip
of a Father
who has also formed
the keyhole.

My brother is the Door.

I place myself in the
opening He has provided
and He turns me
as He will.

Resonance of key in lock
sounds a click.

He has created an opening
where I fit
to open the awareness of
His Ways,
On which He is the Light.

Captives dance through that which is now
open
Into Freedom.

June 15, 2013
Dublin, Ireland
during worship
Matt.16:19

Brenda VanWinkle, California, USA

Brenda has carried Ireland as a love letter inscribed on her heart since childhood. Raised in great part by her grandfather whose roots were in this land, poetry and song, the love of words and communication were instilled early on. Author, speaker and poet, she and husband Jim make their home in California and are the parents of four children and grandparents of two. Brenda brings a gift of encouragement and prophetic insight as she comes to Ireland with a word of the Lord: FLOURISH!
www.bespokeninternational.com

BRENDA VANWINKLE

GLEE!

Here it comes!
    Here it is!
It's beginning to rain.

Drip becomes drop
as smiles
grow up to become
giggles

whose inevitable destiny
melds into
peals of delighted
rippling
c
a
s
c
a
d
i
n
g

laughter.

Belly gripping,
    Cheeks hurt
        Can't stop or I'll snort

            Glee.
I'm free.
      John 8:36

Brenda Vanwinkle

All poetry submitted by Brenda Vanwinkle can be found in her book, 'Poetry from a Flourishing Land'© 2014

Brendan Creed

A Different View

FLY, FLY, LITTLE BUTTERFLY
IT'S TIME TO TRY OUT YOUR WINGS.
TO DANCE ABOVE THE TREE TOPS
WITH MULTICOLOURED WINGS.

NO MORE COCOON OF SLUMBERED THOUGHTS
BUT PANORAMIC VIEWS
ON THE BREATH OF EACH NEW WIND.
THERE IS A NEW ADVENTURE WITH EVERY FLUTTER OF YOUR WINGS.

LANDING ON A SHADED LEAF
FOR A MOMENTS REPOSE,
THE OLD WORLD NOW LIES BELOW,
A SHADED DANGER WITH COLOURS AGLOW.

IN THE BUSYNESS OF DAY
I MET WITH SNAIL.
HE TALKED OF TROUBLE IN THE UNDERWORLD,
THEN GESTURED ME AWAY.

FLY, FLY LITTLE BUTTERFLY. YOUR TIME TO SHINE HAS COME.

2 Corinthians 5: 17

BRENDAN CREED

Song for Breakthrough in Your Life

```
G              C          GCG
Jesus prepares the Bride of Christ today,
   D          C              G       C    G
repentant sinners who are prepared to change their ways.
EM                   C           GCG
They're washed in the blood that flows from Calvary.
C                  D             GCG
They're formed in the word that sets the captives free.
   D        EM       GCG      D
Holy Spirit, teach us you ways; soften our hearts,
EM                GCG
we need to learn to praise.
C                      AM     D     GCG
   Break free, break free, from a life of slavery.
C                      AM     D     GCG
   Break free, break free, from Satan's tyranny.
EM         AM   EM          AM   EM
You must be born again, you must be born again
C          D                          G
With Jesus the Saviour, the Way, the Truth, the Life.
     C      D       G
   Holy Spirit fall afresh on us.
G         C      G   D              C         GCG
Come Holy Spirit of God, your anointing will break every yoke.
EM              AM      EM              AM
Give thanks. Let us praise him. Give thanks. Let us serve him.
EM           AM
Give thanks. Let us worship.
D                    EM  AM EM    AM      EM
For the fruit of the Spirit is "Love, Joy, Peace, Patience, Kindness,
   AM      EM       AM              D
Goodness, Faithfulness, Gentleness and Self-Control"
```

```
EM   D     EM   D
```
Only believe, only believe.
```
G            EM  G         EM
```
To God be the Glory, to God be the Glory...

Narration

> *Come, Holy Spirit, teach us to be sensitive to your ways. O, you sons and daughters of the most high God, hear and obey his call for your life. Be encouraged. Be filled with Holy Spirit power to awaken an unbelieving world. Be poured out that they may be saved through Jesus, the coming Messiah. For one day, every knee will bow and every tongue confess that Jesus Christ is Lord. Choose, this day, to invite Jesus into your heart. Turn around (repent) and follow him through this life and into eternity..... Selah (pause and think of this)*

This Prayer is an invitation to fast track from a time of searching for something, to a time of discovering that we all are in need of a personal and real, day by day, relationship with the living Jesus Christ. If you call to him, he will answer – really, you too can seek and find....

> *I will not leave you orphans; I will come to you.*
>
> *John 14: 18*

Spiritual Songs, Poems and Prophecies

BRENDAN CREED

ARE YOU GOING TO THE WEDDING FEAST OF THE LAMB?

G   C
Are you going to the Wedding Feast of the Lamb.
    C   G
Have you exchanged your filthy garments?
    EM   AM   D
Are you washed in the Blood of the Lamb (Chorus)
    G   D
Is there enough oil in your Lamp?
   EM   BM
Is your life a song of praise?
   C   AM   D
Do you worship at the feet of the Lamb?
  G   D   EM   BM
O the day will surely come when Jesus will return.
    C   AM   D
He will rule in Jerusalem for a thousand years
  G   D
And those living at that time,
    EM   BM
Those having repented, they will find,
    C   AM   D
Themselves, rising up to meet him in the air.

   G   D   EM   BM
O the new Jerusalem, a city of Gold, ruled by Yeshua, the Father's
C   EM   C
Son . . . It's there that the tribes go up
   G   AM   D
And the Nations shall go to worship the King.
Are you going . . . ?
    G   D
Now if this song is a mystery to you,
   EM   BM
There is something you can do:

```
    C                    AM                      D
Invite Jesus into your heart as Saviour and Lord.
      G              D         EM
With the Holy Spirit as your guide, the map the
     BM            EM        AM        D
Word of God, you will be ready for the Lord's return.
      EM                 C      G                    C
Abba Father may your will be done, MAY YOUR KINGDOM COME
     AM     EM      D
On earth as it is in Heaven.
```

ARE YOU GOING   D   D7

```
 EM                       BM
Blessed are those that are called to the
   EM              BM
Marriage feast of the Lamb.    (X 2)
   EM             BM                EM
Are you going to the Wedding Feast of the Lamb    (X2)
```

Matthew 22: 1-14

Note from Brendan:
This song emerged as a prayer especially for those outside the four walls of the Church. It's an invitation to come just as you are. Jesus has a seat for you. Welcome. You will be prepared for eternity on earth and in Heaven.

Brendan Creed

Bring in a Harvest

```
G                     D                      C
Bring in a Harvest, bring in a harvest. Bring in a harvest, bring in a
D             C
harvest, o my church.
G                      D                D
You did not choose me but I choose you,
        C
bear much fruit, that's what to do.
EM             C
Abide in me and I in you.
 D   G         C            D
Without me you can do nothing.
BM         EM  EM7     D
This is my command t
              C      D     EM
hat you should love one another serve one another
G         D     BM      EM            C
By this will all men know that you are my disciples,
     EM       D     EM      D
If you love one another, serve one another.
```

Bring in a harvest...
```
G                D
The Father sent me and I send you
      C              G           D
in the power of the Spirit to God's word be true
G          D      EM           C       D
Do not fear the arrow that flies by day nor the darkness of night.
BM       EM       C       D       EM            D
For I am with you, the light within you the strength within you.
```

Bring in a harvest....
```
G             D             C              D
Humble yourselves, fall on your knees, seek his face and he will lift you
up.
G      EM  EM7           D      C       D
This is a new day for blessing, for healing for forgiving
                                    G
Bring in a harvest......O my Church hear my call.
```

BRENDAN CREED

THE WAY

COME LET US MAGNIFY THE LORD X2
LET US PRAISE HIM   X2
MAY YOUR SPIRIT REJOICE IN HIM   X2
IN JESUS OUR SAVIOUR X2
COME ALL YOU WHO ARE HEAVILY BURDENED
COME YOU REDEEMED OF THE LORD
COME ALL WHO ARE SEARCHING
JUST COME, COME AS YOU ARE

DID YOU KNOW OF JESUS GIFT OF SALVATION
HE POURED OUT HIS LIFE AS A LIBATION.
THE WAGES OF SIN IS DEATH, YOU KNOW
HE PAID, HE PAID THE PRICE FOR YOU.

JESUS, WE INVITED YOU INTO OUR HEARTS
YOU CAME AS LORD AND SAVIOUR
FILL US WITH YOUR SPIRIT
GUIDE US - ALL THE DAYS OF OUR LIVES.

THERE IS NOW NO CONDEMNATION FOR THOSE
FOR THOSE WHO ARE FOUND IN CHRIST JESUS
GOD CAN DO EXCEEDINGLY ABUNDANTLY.
MORE THAN WE ASK OF HIM

THOUGH THERE ARE GIANTS IN THE LAND WE OVERCOME
WITH THE BLOOD OF THE LAMB   X2
(Spoken) and the word of our testimony....we are the overcomers.

BRENDAN CREED, CO. KILDARE, IRELAND
After 5 years in Cistercian College Roscrea and 7 years of study and work, Brendan felt convicted by the Lord to leave Ireland in 1982 to go on a journey of discovery. After an encounter with God & conviction of sin in Dublin, he was led to seek the Person of the Holy Spirit in Rome, & heard the audible voice of God in Paris, before taking Jesus Christ as his Lord and Saviour in Brisbane University. Christian Communities became Brendan's special interest. He has a heart for worship, prophecy and Biblical understanding of Gods role for Israel.

God's Love

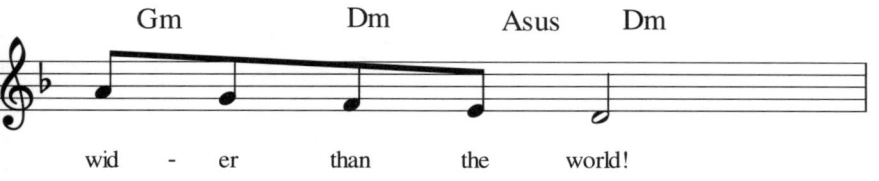

Petra Hake

God's Love God's Love is higher than the stars! Deeper than the deepest sea and wider than the world!

© Petra Hake 2015

Ireland's Heartbeat 2015

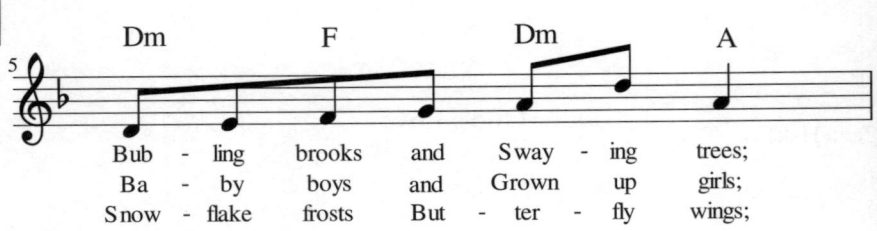

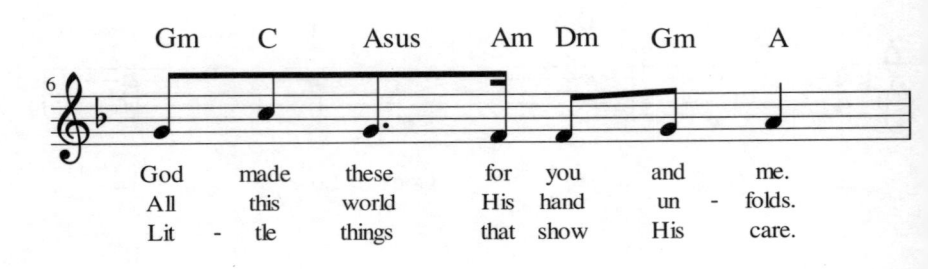

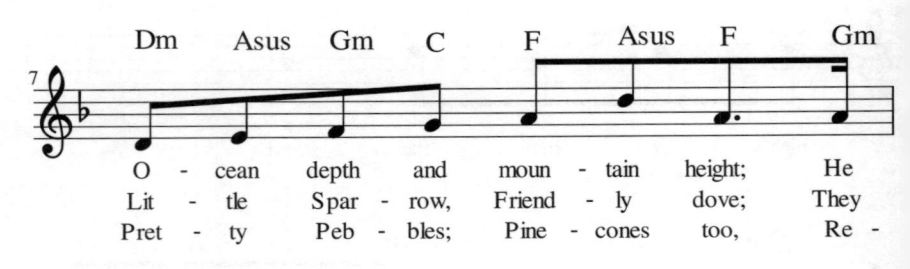

Dm / F / Dm / A

Bub - ling brooks and Sway - ing trees;
Ba - by boys and Grown up girls;
Snow - flake frosts But - ter - fly wings;

Gm / C / Asus / Am Dm / Gm / A

God made these for you and me.
All this world His hand un - folds.
Lit - tle things that show His care.

Dm / Asus / Gm / C / F / Asus / F / Gm

O - cean depth and moun - tain height; He
Lit - tle Spar - row, Friend - ly dove; They
Pret - ty Peb - bles; Pine - cones too, Re -

Gm / Dm / A / Dm

loves with all His Might.
all show forth His Love.
mind that God loves you!

© Petra Hake 2015

With All

Petra Hake / Petra Hake

With all of My Heart; With all of My Soul; With all of My Might: I love you. With Ev-er-y breath; With all that I Am; With all that I have; I Love you. I Love you. I Love you O, will you love Me too? O, Will you love Me too? I Love you.

I died for you. Will you live for Me?
Draw near to Me; I'll draw near to you.
I love you child! Will you come to me?

© Petra Hake 2015

Ireland's Heartbeat 2015

I set you free — Will you Follow Me?
If you seek Me, — I'll be found by you.
Let Me kiss you, — You're so dear to Me.

3. With all of Our hearts; With all of our souls;
with all of our Might: May we love You.
With ev-er-y breath; With all that we are; With all that we have;
May we love You. May we love You. We love You.
O help us love You too. We love You.

© Petra Hake 2015

Why?

The Sons of Korah, Psalm 42
Petra Hake

Voice 1: Why are you so down-cast O_____ my soul?_____

Voice 2: Why are you so down-cast, Why so dis-cour-aged with-in me?_____ O_____ my soul?_____

Put your hope in Why so dis-cour-aged with-in me?_____ God! For I will yet prase Him.

Put your hope in God! For I will ye-t prai-se

© Petra Hake 2003

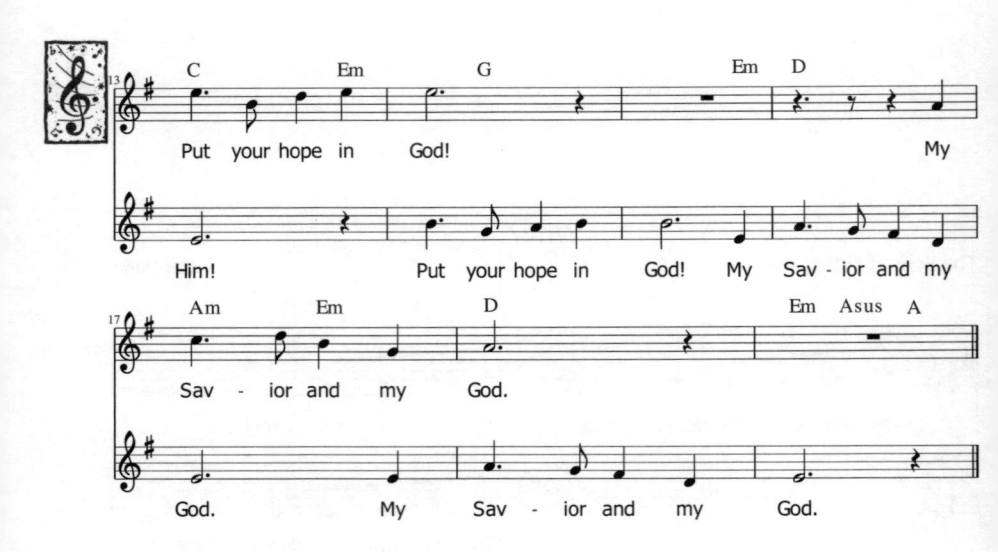

PETRA HAKE, Co. Donegal, Ireland

"I live in a busy household with my husband Brad & our children, Kari, Jona, Ivy Joy, Paul, Natanya, Noah Ann, & David, my mom & dad, Merry & Doug, my siblings Patrick, Joshua & Merry. We are a part of Living Spirit Ministries, In'tl. We like to sing & play music together, and are available for children's ministry, speaking, and special music events. Please feel free to use my songs non-commercially in churches, outreach and so forth." shayassong@gmail.com

Spiritual Songs, Poems and Prophecies

If You Want A Happy Song

Merry Bradley

Petra Hake

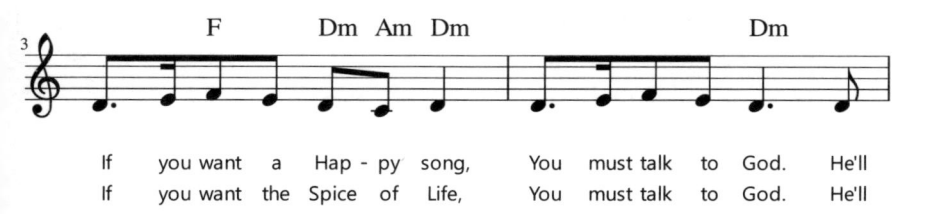

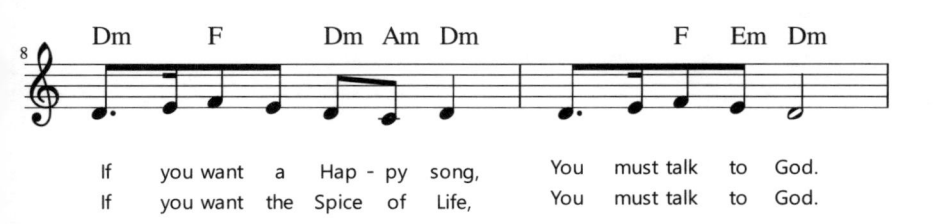

If you want a Happy song, You must talk to God.
If you want the Spice of Life, You must talk to God.

If you want a Happy song, You must talk to God. He'll
If you want the Spice of Life, You must talk to God. He'll

put it in your heart it will be a su-per sta - rt
flip you up-side-down He'll give you a roy-al cro - wn!

If you want a Happy song, You must talk to God.
If you want the Spice of Life, You must talk to God.

© Merry Bradley & Petra Hake 2003

Ireland's Heartbeat 2015

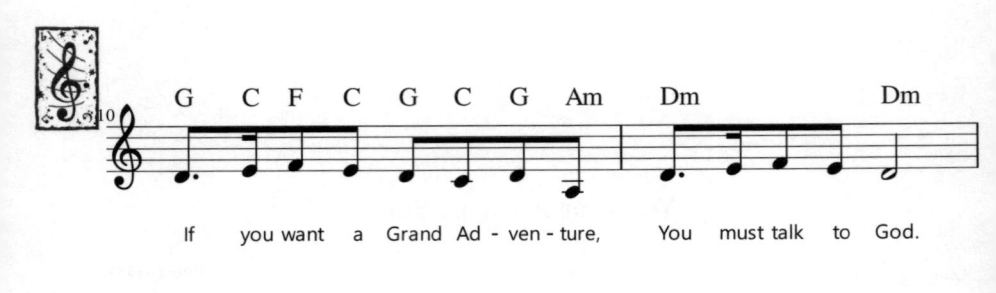

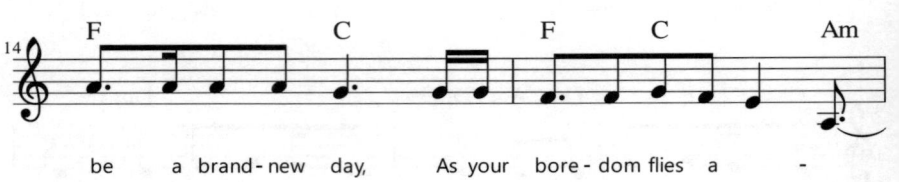

If you want a Grand Adventure, You must talk to God.

If you want a Grand Adventure, You must talk to God. It will be a brand-new day, As your boredom flies away! If you want a Grand Adventure You must talk to God!

© Merry Bradley & Petra Hake 2003

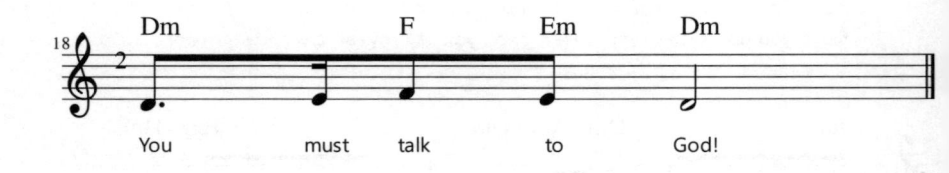

Spiritual Songs, Poems and Prophecies

Prayer to Holy Spirit

Merry Bradley Petra Hake

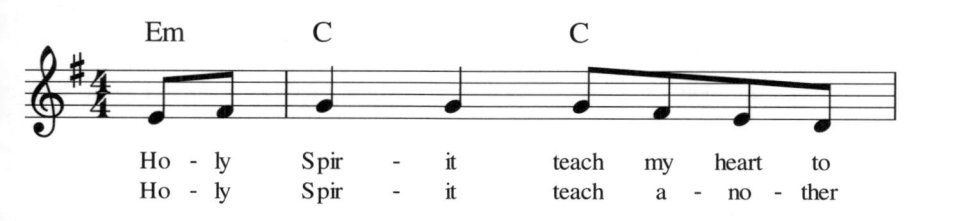

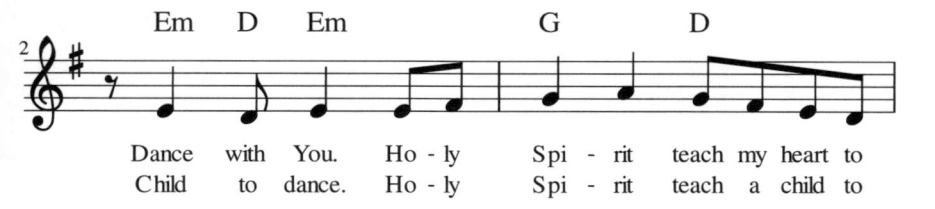

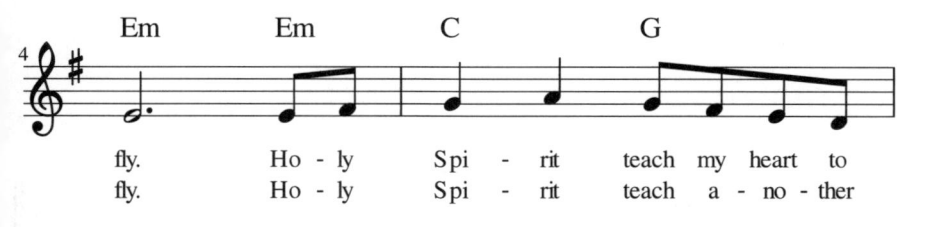

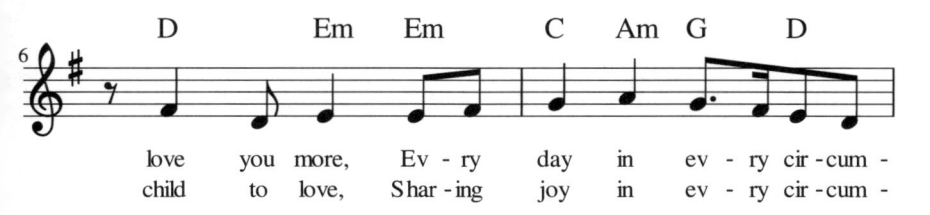

Holy Spirit teach my heart to
Holy Spirit teach another

Dance with You. Holy Spirit teach my heart to
Child to dance. Holy Spirit teach a child to

fly. Holy Spirit teach my heart to
fly. Holy Spirit teach another

love you more, Ev'ry day in ev'ry circum-
child to love, Sharing joy in ev'ry circum-

© Merry Bradley and Petra Hake 1999

Em Em C Am D Em
stance. My Com - fort - er to - ge - ther we dance; My
stance.
C Em Em C
Com - fort - er we fly, My Com - fort - er to -
Em Em C Am7 D Am
ge - ther we love! Shar - ing joy in ev - ry cir - cum -
D.C. al Coda
1.2.
Em Em Em
stance. sta - nce shar - ing
C D Am D Em
joy in ev - ry cir - cum - stance.

MERRY BRADLEY

DRAW CLOSE

Alone in the darkness I call out to You.
I need You here now in my lightless black night.
My heart has been broken with grief and with fright.
So sorry for turning away, make me new.

Draw Close in all you do,
When heavy burdens come.
Cry out and beat your drum!
And I will never go,
Because I love you so;
I gave My all for you.

My song, it was taken from my jail cell!
O help me to tear all these prison cells down.
In faith, not by sight, we face what befalls,
Although it's a blast from the devil's own hell.

Draw Close in all you do,
When heavy burdens come.
Cry out and beat your drum!
And I will never go,
Because I love you so;
I gave My all for you.

Psalm 107:13-14

MERRY BRADLEY, Co. DONEGAL, IRELAND
Merry and her family have returned to the land of her ancestors to minister with Living Spirit Ministries Int'l. She says, "My happiness is in sharing the Good News that Jesus spoke to a sinner, 'I tell you with certainty, today you will be with me in Paradise.' There are no hopeless cases. This Good News is for sinners only. We want you to know that we are ready, willing, and wishing to proclaim the greatness of God wherever we may be permitted, because we want no one to be left behind." Contact Merry at:

merrychristmasivana96@gmail.com

PRINCESS LEWA

Thank God, I'm Free!

I came to live in the
  Land of Milk and Honey.
To my family back home
  – In need – I could send money.

But when I arrived, subjected
  To mercy of my employer's hand,
I was stripped of identity
  In a foreign land.

No passport, no money,
  No freedom to tell –
I was alone and scared
  In my living hell.

Beaten, abused,
  Slept and ate off the floor,
Watched every moment,
  Hidden behind a closed door.

Per-chance, a church man
  Came to that door,
Telling me miracles
  I could believe for.

I saw in his eyes,
  Joy, hope and care.
With this man by my side,
  Escaping, I dare.

I whispered my ordeal.
  He took me by the hand.
He walked me out of captivity
  Into the Promised Land.

Now, my identity intact,
  My freedom I embrace.
I've walked down the aisle,
  Pure, refined, in white lace.

Together we've searched
  For the lost and broken,
Obeying God's word of Love
  That He has spoken.

I wake every day
  To the sound of birds chirpin.'
I thank God, I'm free –
  Of His love, I am certain.

Hebrews 13: 3

PRINCESS LEWA, IRELAND

Princess is one of a number of people who suffered capture into modern-day slavery. Ireland is a destination, source, and transit country for women, men, and children subjected to sex trafficking and forced labour. Most forced labour victims are found in domestic labour, restaurant and agricultural work. An anti human trafficking unit has been set up in Ireland. 'Blue blindfold' asks the public not to close their eyes to human trafficking, but on seeing anything suspicious, to call Crimestoppers 1800 25 20 25 or email blueblindfold@garda.ie

TRANSLATED BY R. SEATHRÚN MAC ÉIN

IS IONTACH GRÁS (IRISH LANGUAGE VERSION OF "AMAZING GRACE")

Is iontach grás – nach binn an fhuaim –
A shlánaigh trú mar mé:
Do fuarthas mé nuair bhíos amú;
Bhíos dall ach dom is léir.

'S é'n grás a mhúin dom uamhan croí
'S an grás scaip m'eagla uaim;
An grásta sin dob' ola'r chroí
San uair chreid mé ar dtús.

Is iomaí saothar, baol is dol
Trí'r thángas slán folláin:
'S é'n grás a thug mé slán 'n fhaid seo
'S an grás a threorós slán.

Do gheall an Tiarna maitheas dom;
'nA Bhriathar dóchasaím.
Mo Sciath is mo chuid É féin
Ar feadh mo shaoil de shíor.

'S nuair theipfeas ionam fuil is feoil
Is scarfas m'anam uaim'
Beidh agam fós laistigh den fhéil
Síorbheatha aoibhinn buan.

Nuair bheimid thall deich míle bliain
Gealruithneach mar an ghréin,
Beidh oiread ama 's bhí ar dtús
Le bheith ag moladh Dé.

Published four times in papers and hymn books, the last time in a booklet to accompany a CD of hymns and carols issued by the Church of Ireland society Cumann Gaelach Na hEaglaise. (The English version is on page 318)

R. Seathrún Mac Éin

Will You Dare to Follow Jesus?

Will you dare to follow Jesus, whate'er the cost may be;
Though you go before a firing squad or hang upon a tree?
Will you dare to follow Jesus, though you perish for His sake?
Will you follow, follow Jesus and never Him forsake?

Chorus:
Yes, I'll dare to follow Jesus, whate'er the cost may be;
I shall follow, follow Jesus, because He died for me.

2 Cor 11: 22-28

Previously published in an issue of CHURCH IN CHAINS magazine.

R. Seathrún Mac Éin, Dublin, Ireland

R. Seathrún (born 1944, born again c.1950) is the younger son of the late Rev. Canon Richard Bird, Rector of Delgany, Co. Wicklow, who helped to compile the 1960 Church Hymnal of the Church of Ireland. Educated at St. Andrew's College Dublin and Trinity College Dublin, Seathrún is now a free-lance journalist and book translator, and gives private tuition in languages. Committee Member of Cumann Gaelach na hEaglaise and, until recently, Church in Chains. He attends Apostolic Church. Studies apologetics: he is convinced that Christians can and must (see 1 Peter 3:15) be prepared to answer non-Christian (e.g. atheist) arguments.

MARGARET BOLES

AT THE BUS STOP

She waited at the bus stop with her buggy
And I was relieved to see
He waited with her, too ~
The child was obviously their own,
For there's something poignant
About a Filipino nanny
Caring for our European children
Knowing she's working for money
To send to her own children
That she's left back home.

We waited an unusually long time,
At the bus stop, today.

Deuteronomy 27:19

WET EVENING ON THE HA'PENNY BRIDGE

A huddle of plastic and cardboard,
Afraid, I scurry by
A Levite, no Samaritan, I.

Luke 10: 32-33

Published in
The Candlestick, Riposte, Books Ireland New Writing, & Modern Woman

MARGARET BOLES

I Want To Be Young Again!

I do not want to be old and grey,
I want to be young and gay!
I want to be young again with my baby on my knee,
And all the world would say well done!
When they saw me with my son
Or daughter on my knee,
In all the world we did never see
Such a baby as she or he,
And I could bask in their reflected glory,
And forget the birth so gory,
Were I young again with my baby on my knee!

*Like arrows in the hand of a warrior,
So are the children of one's youth.*

Psalm 27: 4 NKJV

MARGARET BOLES

No Parking!

If
I park in
A "No Parking" lot
I would be
Embarrassed, at least
And probably
Impoverished
When I had to pay
The fine!

But
If we park
With our old resentments,
Remain in our old quarrels,
We will be
Diminished,
Embarrassed,
When discovered by God.
For these things
Hurt us even more
When we hold onto them,
However innocent!

NO PARKING!
MOVE ALONG, NOW!

James 1: 19-20

MARGARET BOLES

BLOSSOMS ON THE BIN

Almond blossom, or is it Cherry
Has fallen like a dust of snow
On the green bin, the black bin
In the yard, outside the kitchen window.

It cheers my soul; it brightens the dull backwater
Of the otherwise cheerless vista
Looking out at stone wall, old windows and some planks
That could come in handy.....

And the green wooden masterpiece
Of the kennel my husband made
For the dog who won't sleep
Outside at night;

(And a kennel in a yard,
However comfortable, is outside,
She'd much prefer some one's bed
For it's company she craves.)

A sudden gust of wind
Signals March breezes soon
And the blossoms shower down again
A glorious spring confetti,
Baptizing the yard again,
While sparrows, finches
Sing a springtime song.

Habakkuk 3:17

MARGARET BOLES

IMPORTANT PEOPLE

There's a wonderful name in Gaelic
For someone who has a handicap
'Duine le Dia' they are referred to,
"A person of or with God".
So well describes it, for they
Have a marvellous joy for life,
And a trusting smile for all,
They bring us back
To the simpler things in life,
More precious, more real!

'Whoever receives one little child like this in My name receives Me.'
Matthew 18: 5 NKJV

MARGARET BOLES, DUBLIN, IRELAND
Margaret discovered in herself an ability to write poetry when her family were still small. Her writing hobby prompted her, following the death of her mother, to gain a BA (English, Philosophy, Women's Studies) and an MA in Women's Studies from University College Dublin. This she funded by a part-time return to her earlier career of nursing, through agency work, which she still enjoys. Her work has been published widely in small press magazines, and via the Candlestick read on UBC Radio.

Gordon, Business as Usual

Gordon Cochran, born with an intellectual disability, with almost no speech, travelled every day by bus and train, dressed as a business man because that's how his daddy dressed. And everywhere he went, people became his friends. Though Gordon had many problems, the story of his life rings with joy, a story his sister, Ruth Chipperfield, poignantly shares in the biography, *'Gordon, Business as Usual'*. Ruth has kindly given permission for extracts of her book to be published in this anthology.

Do this in Memory.

On Sundays in our church at Fairview, in north Dublin, the first morning service . . . was what we called the Breaking of Bread. This was Holy Communion, in its simplest form. Everybody who was there, who was a follower of Jesus, was invited to join in by eating a little piece of bread and drinking a sip of wine . . .

My mother began to speculate that, since he couldn't fully understand communion, Gordon might not be eligible to join in; he certainly hadn't been invited to. The leaders of the church – that is our local church, not The Church Universal – hadn't had this issue to consider before, so when Gordon's parents raised it there was a lot of prayer and of reading relevant parts of the Bible. In the end the decision was made, perfectly and simply. Gordon did what Jesus had asked him to do.

One problem: Gordon has the brain development of a tiny child... but Jesus said

> 'Let the little children come to me, and do not hinder them, for the kingdom of heaven belongs to such as these'.

Another problem: Gordon can't do theological discussions. He'll never understand the Gospel, fully... but Jesus said,

> 'I tell you the truth, unless you change and become like little children, you will never enter the kingdom of heaven'.

A third problem: Gordon can't pray proper prayers, or ask for forgiveness, it's too abstract. When he has hurt his mother, he offers to shake hands. His mind can't see Jesus... but Jesus said,
> 'Whoever comes to me I will never drive away'.
> Matthew 19:14, Matthew 18:3, John 6:37.

Well, every word in the Bible is there for a purpose, for our instruction, our comfort, our joy, our reproof, our morality, our relationships, our work ethic, our delight in creation, our eternal salvation, our earthly peace. Could God have overlooked the Gordons of this world? Of course not. Gordon is covered by many more writings than those I've quoted above.

My kid brother had learned, up to the full of his understanding, from his mother and father, that Jesus loved him. Her singing to him when he was little had, while he was yet unaware, filled his heart with the knowledge of God. He started to take bread and wine, in full and glorious fellowship.

While on this question of limited understanding, I remember visiting a very elderly friend in Portrush, in Co Antrim. He had had a long life as a missionary, travelling the world. His wife, a brilliant and Godly woman, was deep in dementia. Ernest Lloyd and I talked about dementia. His beloved Jessie couldn't hold a conversation with him, she couldn't ask a question, or answer one.

Where was she?

In spiritual terms, how can a person who has an intellectual disability be taught about God's love, in a way that gets past that dense curtain, and means something to them?

The Bible has the answer to that:
> He (God) has put his Spirit in our hearts... The Spirit helps us in our weakness... He (God) who searches our hearts knows the mind of the Spirit, because the Spirit intercedes. God is revealed to us by His Spirit.
> 2 Corinthians 1:22, Romans 8:26, 1 Corinthians 2:10

God's Holy Spirit can speak to the infant, to the person with brain-injury, to the one who is demented, with perfect clarity according to their need.

So, that was Gordon sorted.

I don't mean that trivially. Answers to the questions were found in God's Word, and that was enough. Will and Lydia had peace in the deepest parts of their minds, and their spirits were at rest.

WHERE, O DEATH, IS YOUR STING?

On Thursday 23rd July, 1992, five days after the wedding, my dad phoned, saying that the nursing home had advised us to come in. So we went and sat with my mother. Such stillness, such tiny breaths. We chatted quietly as we waited for a long time, then I listened, and said, 'I think she has died.' Before we left, Will bent over, kissed Lydia, and murmured 'Goodbye, Beloved'.

> *In righteousness I shall see your face; when I awake, I shall be satisfied with seeing your likeness.*
> *Psalm 17.*

When Gordon came home that evening, my dad had to explain to him that mummymummy had gone to be with Jesus.

The funeral was two days later, on Saturday. Lydia was never impressed by traditions, either she didn't know of them or she just brushed them aside. Her wish, her instruction, was that her coffin would not be brought into the church for her funeral. So we left it outside. Some of her family members were unsettled by this; we had overlooked that there was no opportunity for them to honour her by sharing the carrying of her coffin. This was remedied later, when they carried her body to the grave for burial. We were grateful for the way in which these family members honoured Lydia. They had loved her and they shared our sense of loss.

Gordon sat with us at the front of the church, not noticeably grief-stricken, but quiet and solemn. Our life-long friend, Fred Stephens, conducted the service. I spoke about my mother, a high privilege. I think my dad would have loved to do it, but either didn't feel up to the challenge, or - more likely – he chose to give it to me. At the burial ground we sang hymns of praise, we prayed, and Lydia's body was interred.

Now I had to explain to Gordon the two complementary truths about his mother's death. I told him that - as he knew - she had become very old and tired and she had lots of pains. So Jesus knew it was time for her to go to heaven. She didn't need her old body because Jesus made her a beautiful new one, and she would never be old and tired again. Because she belonged to Jesus, she would be properly well and happy always. That's why we put her old body into the ground.

Whether my theology helped Gordon I can't judge, but if you asked him 'where's mummy now?' he answered 'He'ben'. On the other hand if you drove past the graveyard, Gogo would point towards it with a casual
thumb, 'Mummymummy'.

. . . It was exactly one week after Abigail's wedding, and lots of wedding guests were with us at the funeral, and they had photos! There was no pall of gloom, it was a fine day, and we simply revelled in the love of friends and family. It was exactly the sort of function that was to Gordon's taste. Funerals never made him sad. There were mercies in his disability.

Epilogue

The engine driver yawned. He enjoyed his job, but sometimes it was just too peaceful. Nothing really happens when you're in your cab, rolling along. That's because of all training you get, nothing's meant to happen. It goes like clockwork. For far too long sometimes. He'd really like to get out and go for a walk, the sun was shining.

It was a Bank Holiday Monday, and there were lots of people out and about.

The journey seemed interminable. He'd come from Cork through Mallow and Limerick Junction, which wasn't a town at all, it was in the middle of nowhere. He had trundled through Thurles and Portlaoise, charming places, no doubt, but not to a tired train driver who wanted to get home. Kildare was next and eventually Heuston, Dublin.

He liked Kildare, because next stop would be Dublin, and he liked the long railway embankment running beside the Curragh. He could see in all directions, and on the wide plain he sometimes saw strings of racehorses being exercised.

The racecourse on that day was empty and quiet, but he enjoyed imagining it full of crowds and excitement as people yelled, sometimes in despair, at their favourite, 'Come On!'

Just past Kildare a few cars had turned off the M7, along the road towards the embankment. One car was parked surprisingly close, and people were relaxing with a picnic. The train left Kildare railway station, picked up speed and began to come closer to the picnickers, and the low rumble grew louder, and you could feel it with your feet.

One of the men in the little group leapt up, all a-quiver, galvanised with excitement. He was a short fellow, but somehow he looked ten feet tall. He sped over to the embankment and he stood there, waving his arms, almost levitating, and shouting as the train drew level.

The driver saw him. His hand went to the horn, and he leaned on it. As the sound of the horn tore through the air, out of the engine window stretched an arm and the driver waved, and waved, and his train sped on.

Settled back in his seat, the driver was smiling.

'That' he said to himself, 'was Gordon'.

> God be in my head, and in my understanding;
> God be in my eyes, and in my looking;
> God be in my mouth, and in my speaking;
> God be in my heart, and in my thinking;
> God be at mine end, and at my departing.
> *Sarum primer, 1558*

Gordon, Business as Usual (Ballpoint Press, 2014) is stocked by Footprints bookshops in Dublin and Dun Laoghaire, by the Rathfarnham and Greystones bookshops, and is available online from Amazon.co.uk and biblio.com.

RUTH CHIPPERFIELD, DUBLIN, IRELAND

Ruth has always loved reading, from Enid Blyton's school stories in early childhood, to biography and memoir, literary novels, crime novels and thrillers, and newspapers and the endless riches of the Bible. Her joy and pre-occupation has been with words, reading them and using them. 'Gordon, Business as Usual' was written after major changes in Gordon's life. Ruth is married, with three adult married children, and six grandchildren, aged from four to seventeen.

Email: rchipperfield@hotmail.com

ROBERT CREED

THE TRAIN

The sliding doors of Cork station give way,
To me and my cane and my bags and my fast flowing thoughts,
Which left and right and up and down will stray,
As I am running, running, running, believing that I will make it.

And as brief words fly,
I loosen my grip,
On the arm of a man,
Who brought me on this trip.
Within a breath I grab on to another,
Who with fast paced footsteps will bring me further,
Then by faith, I stretch my leg
Across a vast gap.
On to two steps, I am to touch my toes.
As I lift myself forward the whistle finally blows.

Then nine times a piercing beep
Sends a warning signal through my ears to my brain,
As closing doors behind me creak,
Reminding me that I have only just made the train.

Through a tunnel of darkness the train will go,
As all the time its speed will grow,
Then burst in to a light as bright as day,
A day I pray I soon will fully see.

The beats of train tracks beneath me increase,
As my heart rate and blood pressure begin to decrease,
And I settle in to my seat,
Staying still but feeling movement under my feet.

Familiar announcements then will follow,
Spoken at the same time, today and tomorrow,
When suddenly an old lady will say,
"Where am I going, am I going the right way?"
I respond, "yes you are, and soon you will be home",

As panic gives way because she knows she's not alone.
So we sit and talk as through the country we move,
Passing a vast array of communities,
Carrying out their daily lives.

And is that not what all of us do,
Though we think we are still and being made old,
Time is always being made new
Even when we are doing nothing,
We are still reaching our final destination.

And every day our conscience will announce
That we should love and not violently pounce,
And even through the tunnels, we should trust
That the lord is moving us from dawn in to dusk.

And from dusk to midnight,
In its cold dark hour,
He gave us the moon and stars,
Showing his faithful power,
To always be the light of this world,
Who will never abandon us,
Though the clocks of time will continue to tick.

And as midnight passes, the stars will fade,
As faint colours begin to be laid,
Afar I see a growing golden light amidst the gloom,
As the birds sing a redeeming tune.

With great glory the sun has risen
Spreading oranges, and reds, and yellows across the vast horizon,
Reminding us that in Christ we are made a new creation,
'In Christ, we are the righteousness of God'. What a proclamation!

Though the train for the last time is slowing,
I will never stop moving,
To the bright lights of heaven,
In Christ, I am always pursuing.

Isaiah 45: 7

Robert Creed

Pain

It is here again and shaking my bones,
As I lie heaving, but still and cold.
It is all around my chest now,
And flows down my arm,
To my finger tips as I type these words of woe.

It punctured my skin years ago,
And left behind a wound still bleeding,
And I am still and shocked,
While the knife is violently stabbing.

The wound is too deep to find its end
Or even tell where it began.
It gets uncovered by an innocent hand,
Clueless of the pain and loss relived.

And I lie upon a searing pan,
Full of flashes of heat which takes me back
To a sudden moment when sight was lost,
As light caved in around me.

And the pain is now real again,
With its consequences repeating,
As my world spins fast but I am trapped,
In the deep darkness revealing my loss

Which is right there, on Christ,
As he was nailed to that cross,
And felt my pain like no one else can,
And took it upon himself
So that I don't need to relive it.

And that would be a fitting end,
But what a better person could there be,
Then someone who lost a lot of sight,
To speak to those who cannot see,
To show them the light.

And now the pain grows again,
But I can claim my miracle,
Which is full sight,
Seen as two full circles printed on my heart,
Never to be broken again.

But sometimes it is hard to look forward,
When all feels failed and lost,
So I pray Lord, lead me to that cross
Where you suffered for every unseeing eye,
And show me your light,
So that I will remember
That in the body of Christ, I am a fully seeing member.

> *But he was wounded for our transgressions, he was crushed for our iniquities; upon him was the chastisement that brought us peace, and with his stripes we our healed.*
> *Isaiah 53:5 NIV*

> *'But he said to me, "My grace is sufficient for you, for my power is made perfect in weakness." Therefore I will boast all the more gladly of my weaknesses, so that the power of Christ may rest upon me.'*
> *2 Corinthians 12:9 ESV*

ROBERT CREED

SLEEPING

My mind slows as speech slurs to a standstill.
I feel myself encased in air gently flowing around me.
My arms and legs protest against movement by sticking to soft bed sheets
As sleep beckons me to a land of mystery.

My eyes feel like bags of coal dropping into an endless ocean,
While on infinite nets I cast my cares to touch a sea of unconsciousness,
To catch a dream under a silvery gleam,
Of the moon against the still sky surrounding me.

I hear a muffled sound of murmuring,
Of soft shoes scurrying and hard shoes hurrying,
Numerous colours intertwine and separate,
To reveal a world that my mind will create.

I am in a crowd moved by momentum,
To a room filled with scarlet seats,
Viewing a stage that is bare
Except for a piano and chair,
As I sit in ignorance to see,
What type of tale will be woven for me?

Next, I know that I'm destined to go
On a musical journey into my soul,
As Christ's light shines out from the gloom,
Of a singer saying 'this song is for the broken hearted in the room,
Who wonder if all that has gone wrong could ever be made right again'.

Now I know what is coming –

It is a song which reminds me,
That my sightlessness I can carry,
And then leave behind me,
As sung words flow, God's comfort is tasted,
While he sings, 'In the hands of our Redeemer, nothing is wasted'.*

And as he sings words which unveil
A deeply felt pain from when my eyes closed and failed,
I am gently guided to a greater light provided,
To cause a retch like me to rise into unseen beauty.

As the piano plays, the whitest lights fly,
To fill with colour my still closed eyes,
Dancing through the hardest pain,
Where I receive the greatest healing,
As the light of Gods glory
Can turn blindness into seeing.

The words of the song like a bell rings clear
Through the white lights of the piano,
Which merge with the lights of the stage, and the seats,
And the people, and the roof,
And the dark sky, upon which is resting a silvery moon,
And a soft still sea,
Where my nets retreat.

The red sun then rises,
As light enters my eyes,
As I rise to a new day,
Filled with God's glorious surprises.

Isaiah 60:1

* Jason Gray was the singer singing 'Nothing is wasted'.

ROBERT CREED

AMAZING

Awesome power, stretching beyond any linguistic boundaries,
Mighty to save sinners searching for a better way,
Abundantly able to heal and restore
Zealous and propelling upwards the broken, weak and poor,
Is and was and always will be
No longer unknown but my all sufficiently loving God

> *"but I will restore you to health and heal your wounds", declares the Lord...*
>
> *Jeremiah 30:17 NIV*

> *The Lord is close to the broken hearted and saves those who are crushed in spirit.*
>
> *Psalm 34:18 NIV*

ROBERT CREED

The Sound of Ireland

On Europe's western fringe,
Between an ocean and a sea,
Lies a tiny island,
Whose sound has always enthralled me.

Irelands' many different instruments,
Blend across from shore to shore,
Becoming a soundscape as beautiful as her landscape,
But have you really heard it before?

Have you heard the flute and whistle hop?
Or the fiddle and concertina down the octave drop,
Or the rousing passion of pipes and accordion,
Or the most gentle, deeply tranquil plucking of the harp.

Ascending through the reels and jigs,
Have you ever had that minute
When a slow air goes further than words,
And touches your heart, healing pain that is in it?

But where is this music going?
I am sitting, jaw dropped at a concert or session
But in my heart there is deep yearning,
Lord, bring our music unto You.

Would you make it bud and blossom in your Holy Spirit?
Would you cleanse it through the blood of your son?
And redeem it through the cross?
Would you make it a pure praise unto You?

As I worship You in church,
I see how singing voices and guitar chords
Can be filled with a sound that rises like an eagle,
Our sound, which longs to truly live in Christ,
But in this room there is just one tin whistle.

Lord, You have made us new in You,
Would You take the traditional melodies of our people,
And also make them new in You,
For the hearts behind the music are looking for life.

LORD, I INVITE YOU INTO THE SOUND OF IRELAND.

> *Praise the Lord with the harp; make music to him on the ten-stringed lyre. Sing to him a new song; play skilfully, and shout for joy.*
>
> Psalm 33:2–3 NIV

> *Praise him with tambourine and dance; praise him with strings and pipe!*
>
> Psalm 150: 4 ESV

ROBERT CREED, CORK, IRELAND

"I was born in 1991. I attended a school for the blind and visually impaired and there I got introduced to music and poetry. Ever since that moment music has meant a great deal to me. I play the button accordion, tin whistle, melodeon, low whistle and I sing. Poetry became yet another way for me to express myself. After a traumatic year I lost most of my eye sight. However, I found that my faith combined with music and poetry has been instrumental in bringing me through my darkest days."

The Voice of the Young

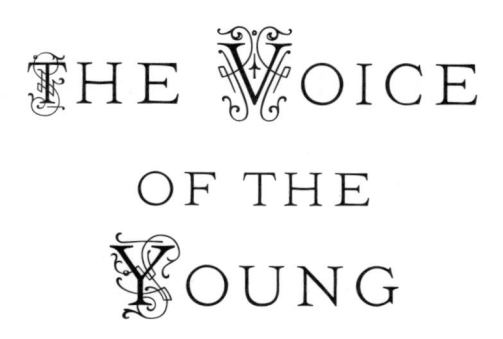

> . . . *"Let the children come to me. Don't stop them! For the Kingdom of God belongs to those who are like these children. I tell you the truth, anyone who doesn't receive the Kingdom of God like a child will never enter it."*
> *(Jesus)*
> *Mark 10: 14-15* NLT

A competition was set for children and youths, asking for creative writing on the subject of *'A day in the life of a school kid'* On the following pages are competition winners - Irish, American, African and Romanian young people, living in Ireland, as well as second and even fourth generation Irish living abroad. A whole class from Belfast also entered a poem they had written together. Collectively, these competition winners' works give a youthful view of life in 2015.

WELL DONE TO YOU ALL!

HOLLY MAE CHIPPENDALE

SCHOOL IS NOT A WASTE OF TIME

Monday to Friday at school,
Yay it's time for literacy,
And oh it's time for math,
And at lunchtime we have a laugh.
After this no time to miss,
Topic and Science.
We draw a castle with no hassle,
With electricity in our circuit,
To make a light bulb shine.
I know the teachers are there for me,
So you can see,
School is not a waste of time.

HOLLY MAE CHIPPENDALE, DERBYSHIRE, ENGLAND

"My name is Holly Mae Chippendale.
I am 9yrs old and I love Drama and I like to have fun with it by referring to myself as Drama Girl. I also love reading and my pug Mr Boogles.
My Mum's Nana came from Ireland, but I haven't been there yet."

Ivy Joy Hake, Donegal, Ireland

Hi, my name is Ivy Joy.
I am 10 years old, turning 11 in April.
I like to read books and hug my dog and my cat.

My Dog Hugs

My Dog Hugs
My Dog Licks
We call Him
Mister Hug a Mix

The Dog Who Chased the Neighbours Around

One day my dog went outdoors;
And chased the neighbours far and wide.
They screamed, and yelled for me to catch him -
I tried until they decided to hide.
Though I must add, my dog is quite kind;
When company comes, he loses his mind.

The story behind the poem . . .
"On Saint Patrick's Day this year, our dog ran up to town and met a group of teenagers, some of whom he knows. Then, my mom met them, and ended up inviting between 25 and 40 teens to our house for tea! They came over, and had fun. About 10 or 15 of them came back later, and as they were halfway up the drive, the dog came running up to meet them – and several of the girls decided to run from him – I think in jest, but then my dog chased them more!"

SOFIA MAHER

A MEADOW IN IRELAND

A green meadow covers the mighty land.

There isn't a shadow in sight,
surrounding the flowers so bright.
Blue, green, yellow, tourquoise, and red.
Tommy under a tree, waiting for his story to be read.

The grass in the meadow is waving hello
The spring breeze is telling it which way to go.
The sky is as blue as a shining sea.
"Look, look at this meadow surrounding me!"

SOFIA MAHER, LAAKEN, BRUSSELS
"My name is Sofia. I am 10 years old. I go to the European School in Laaken, Brussels. I like playing with my friends, playing on my ipad and making up stories. My favourite subjects at school are English and Maths. I also learn French, Czech, and Irish languages
My dad is from Kilkenny in Ireland. I love to visit my family in Ireland. I have 3 uncles, a grand aunt, and two cousins living there. My favourite Irish expression is 'I'm grand'."

EMMA DUFFY

My School Day Song

Up early in the morn
Get my uniform on
Bia reidh don am lóin
See ya Mum, I'm gone

Meet friends on the bus
No-one's cooler than us
Catching-up is a must
Latest music is discussed, 'cause

[chorus]
Going to school is so cool
Le chéile, rang ar siúl,
Skip a class, be a fool
Say it out loud "School Rules"

Bell has rung
Time to run
Teacher's checkin
Homework's done

Laugh with friends
When break is on
Stories and trends
Plus dance and song, 'cause

[chorus]

Learning's the way
Different things each day
Teacher guides our way
In our hearts she'll stay

PE's a laugh
For the kids and staff
Make n Do and Craft
So much fun in art, 'cause

[chorus]

Read, spell and write
Making sure they're right
Math's often a fright
Science sheds a light

Fun games and thrills
and learning new skills
Hearts and minds we fill
Memories always will, 'cause

[chorus]

Day's too short
Now we all depart
Another day will start
Lift my School Day's heart, 'cause

[Last chorus]

EMMA DUFFY, NAVAN, CO. MEATH

"My name is Emma. I'm a 12 year old, 6th Class student in primary school. While I enjoy a wide range of activities including singing, dancing, acting, playing piano, art and sports, my greatest interest is in creative writing where I can use my imagination and love of music and drama to produce stories, poems and songs. My parents and teachers give me every support and encouragement to write stories and verses. I think that writing is fun and is a wonderful way of creating something that, hopefully, others can enjoy."

JOSHUA PETER BRADLEY

A STORMY DAY

The sky is grey
The wind is blowing,
I don't think it will be snowing,
We stay inside today,
Thinking of something to play.
We found some interesting games.
We played Monopoly, Poker, and Cross-word.
We tried to stop from getting bored.
Then the clouds went away,
And the wind stopped blowing,
And we all went out to play.

JOSHUA PETER BRADLEY, CO. DONEGAL, IRELAND
"I'm Joshua. There are 14 people in my family and most of us are learning to play an instrument and we are going to have a band. Kari and I are going to play the drums and guitar. I like reading my Bible and going on walks to the beach. My sister Petra likes going on walks. I like playing board games with my family and it will be a lot of fun having a band when we get it started."

LAURA FARRELLY

IRELAND

Oh Ireland is a beautiful land.
Where green grass grows
where willow trees stand.

Among the branches that once
thatched the little cottages
that dotted the country side,
is not where from God you can hide.

For God sees you everywhere.
He knows each and every
strand of your hair.
He is the way the truth and the life
and he has made many a beautiful sight.

Among his wonderful creation are my friends.
They will stay my friends to all ends.
Although they don't all know God properly,
I'm sure they'll come to love he.

For he is the one who created water and sand
He created Ireland.

Luke 12: 7

LAURA FARRELLY, Co. LEITRIM, IRELAND
"My name is Laura Farrelly. I was born in Ireland in 2003. I live in lovely Leitrim with my mum Ailish. I have a pony, two dogs, a cat, a budgie and a gerbil. I gave my life to God when I was 5 years old."

SAMUEL McNABB

Bully!!!

Hey mister bully
You're really really woolly
I take three steps and you got me in a
Nudgy

When I walk home
You step in front of me
And when I try to step past
You make a big lash

And then when I get home
I think it's all safe then I check my phone
And there's a big lie
You said in Viber to the whole class
That I was a bully
That made you step in glass

Then after an hour or two I go to bed with nothing to do
So I start to think. Think about you

And how much trouble
I will be in if the teacher found out
What you said on Viber

So when I go back to school
It will start all over
Because there's no one to talk to
Because your dad is in the school

Say "No!" to Bullying

SAMUEL MCNABB, DUBLIN, IRELAND

"My name is Sam. I am 12 years old. I live in Dublin and I have one brother who is 8. I like playing the Bodhrán and my drums, cooking and playing with my friends outside. I enjoy travelling and would love to go to Egypt when I'm older. I wrote the poem 'Bully' because Bullying is such a problem for children my age."

MÉABH NÍ SCATHGHAIL

A DAY IN THE LIFE OF A SCHOOL KID

In the morning, I'll get ready,
Laces tied, feet steady,
I'll walk the road and greet the day,
My school-day's free, I've no price to pay.

I reach the yard and join my friend,
We are only children, without much to comprehend,
My mind begins to drift and wander,
Is a school kid's life different yonder?

Do they greet the day with happiness and glee?,
Is a school kid what they want to be?
Do they make it to school safe and sound?,
To get there must they hide, blend in with the crowd?

Is their road to school as smooth as mine?,
Are girls allowed, must they pay a fine?
In countries such as Pakistan and Iraq,
Can school kids walk home without fear of an attack?

All these are questions I must ask,
All these things happen, hidden behind a mask.
I know how difficult some school kid's lives can be,
I know how lucky I am to be me.

MÉABH NÍ SCATHGHAIL, DUBLIN, IRELAND

"My name is Méabh. I am 12 years old. I was born in Dublin.
"Méabh is ainm dom. Tá mé dhá bhliain déag d'aois.
Rugadh agus togadh mé i mBáile Átha Cliath.

"I chose to highlight the difference between my school day and the school day of children in other countries in my poem, 'A Day in the Life of a School Kid' because I believe that it is so much easier for children here in Ireland to go to school and receive an education than in other countries.

"Roghnaigh mé an difir idir mo lá scoile agus lá scoile daltaí i tír difriúil a leiriú i mo dhán, 'A Day in the Life of a School Kid' toisc go gceapaim go bhfuil rudaí i bhfad níos éasca anseo ná in áiteanna éagsúla.

"I enjoyed writing my poem tremendously. I hope to be a writer when I grow up."
"Bhain mé an taitneamh as an dán a scríobh. Ba mhaith liom a bheith i mo scríbhneoir nuair atá mé níos sine."

Spiritual Songs, Poems and Prophecies

JONA FAITH HAKE

I Love You Jesus!

Jona Faith Hake   Jona Faith Hake

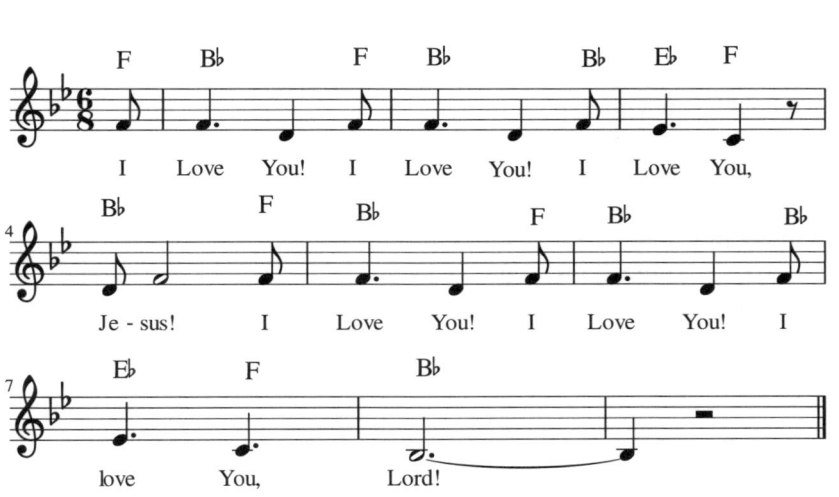

I Love You! I Love You! I Love You, Je-sus! I Love You! I Love You! I love You, Lord!

JONA FAITH HAKE, COUNTY DONEGAL, IRELAND

"Hi, I'm Jona. I like to paint. I enjoy painting birds the most, with lots of colourful flowers.
Climbing trees is a lot of fun, because I get to show off that I can climb trees well. I like reading books and cuddling animals, because they are fluffy and sweet. I wrote the song, 'I love you Jesus' when I was only five years old, and it has been a family favourite ever since!"

LYNDA COLLINS

MONDAY MORNING

Monday morning, lots of maths and P.E.
Tuesday morning, don't forget your lunch.
Wednesday morning, it's computer time.
Thursday morning, five hours to go.
Friday morning, time to do our tests.
Saturday morning, time to text my friends.
Sunday morning, I'm ready for church.
Monday morning, back to school again.

LYNDA COLLINS, CO. CORK, IRELAND

"My name is Lynda. I am 11 years old. I like to bake, go on walks with my friends, do maths and read. I live in Cobh. I would love to be a teacher when I'm older. I wrote the poem Monday Morning with my friends, Kelly Walsh and Lucy Kensall, because it's what we love about our week."

YEAR 9 STUDENTS, ASHFIELD SCHOOL

THE SONG OF ASHFIELD

I am the school bell that peals in Avoneil.
I am C.S. Lewis exploring my wardrobe.
I am the crepes in St. George's Market on Saturday morning.
I am the ghost in Scrabo Tower.
I am a tick-tock in the Albert Clock.
I am the fireworks display at the Odyssey.
I am the gills on the Salmon of Knowledge in the Lagan.
I am Cavehill, where the harsh winds blow.
I am the oil dripping onto the boats in the shipyard.
I am the granite in the Mourne Mountains, covered in a haunting mist.
I am a neighbour of Van the Man's on Cypress Avenue.
I am Madam George going South on North Street.
I am the club swung by Rory McIlroy on Sunday afternoon.
I am the lace on the boot of George Best.
I am the lost suitcase at George Best Airport.
I am a bird following the plane's vapour trail.
I am the smell of cinnamon at Christmas at the City Hall.
I am a mashed Comber spud with gravy.
I am the unsolved mystery in Mount Stewart.
I am the Titanic slipping down an April sea.
I am an iceberg floating in my memory.
We are Samson and Goliath,
The yellow cranes,
Waiting for our ship to return.
I am Belfast,
And Belfast is me.

> This poem was written as a collaborative piece by a whole class of year 9 students from Ashfield school, Belfast. Frank Galligan ran three workshops with Suzanne Simpson's class, during which time he taught them 'The Song of Amergin' in the original Gaelic, as well as in translation, as inspiration for the piece they wrote about living in East Belfast.

Karis Hake

The Master's Plan

In pink and purple, red and gold,
The beauty of the sky unfolds;
And think, more beauty would be still,
If we would do the Master's will.

He meant more beauty, far to be,
But they would only selfish be
And so we live in barren lands,
Because we left the Master's plan.

But He has made a way for us,
He gave his Son to die for us.
So we could meet Him face to face
And all His love we could embrace.

In pink and purple, red and gold,
The beauty of the sky unfolds,
More beauty will engulf this land,
If we follow the Master's plan.

KARIS HAKE

THE BREAKFAST OF A ONE-YEAR-OLD

Dishes flying everywhere,
Mashed potatoes in my hair.
Food for eating: no not me!
Come now let's test gravity-
You shall wear potatoes too!
'Cause I'm in that sort of mood.
The kitchen's in a messy state,
And I now have an empty plate.
Now let's go a different path -
Mom, it's time to take a bath!

KARIS HAKE, COUNTY DONEGAL, IRELAND

"Hi, I'm Kari, I'm 15 years old. I'm a Whovian (Dr. Who fan) and I like to play with my little brother, David, and make him laugh. I like music. My favorite artists are Toby Mac, Newsboys, DCTalk and Petra. I have a pet dog, whom I begged to have for 10 years before I got him. My dog's name is Sir Robin Zelophehad Snuggles Barry Leaf the Dog."

Virginia O'Connor

Memories as Precious as a Jewel

There are typical ingredients to each school day,
That influence us all in a different way
Crossing off the days to the weekend,
Our refill pages pad pages we do send,
Anxiously staring at the clocks,
Sticking together in our flocks
The daily friendly elated teasing,
Rolling our eyes at continuous sneezing,
Running hopelessly to avoid the dreaded late,
But for our friends we always must wait,
The bored chewing of gum, the aimless clicking of pens,
Racing to the lockers, fussing like hens,
Staring out windows, pondering what it all means,
Deciding to work and accomplish our dreams,
The comparisons and questions of who we are
The confusion on how we'll light up our star,
We're told these are the best days of our lives,
Where the lows are easily outnumbered by the highs,
A place where personalities are formed and found,
A place where lifelong friendships are bound
Although we moan, no student can deny,
Our six secondary years really do fly,
Remember to cherish the positives about school,
They are the memories as precious as a jewel

Virginia O'Connor, Dublin, Ireland
"I am an 18 year old student about to do my leaving cert that loves poetry, films and music. I see them as such fascinating forms of expression. I plan to pursue my lifelong ambition and passion of acting. I heard about the competition from my religion teacher and I wrote the poem based on my experience of school."

Melinda Huian

A Day in the Life of a School Kid

Firstly, I think that we are all familiar with this routine. Some of you are grinning right now remembering those days where you and your friends sat at the back of the classroom passing notes to each other (or you can be getting the goose bumps thinking back to all those hours spent studying maths), while others may still even be in these stages. Either way, it seems that we've all found common ground.

A typical day consisted of your alarm blaring at seven in the morning, screaming at you to get up. Let's admit it, it was bad enough rolling over in bed and sticking an arm out from under the warmth of the duvet and then into the cold unforgiving air, never mind actually using up all of your strength and will power to get out of the bed. Gravity just doesn't seem to want to let you go in the morning.

After (hopefully) successfully getting out of bed, you realise that you've used up all your energy reserve. Knowing this, a grunt escapes your mouth in acknowledgement of your parents who are happily eating their food and conversing at the breakfast table, saying 'Good morning son/daughter.'

By the time you have a giant bowl of coco-pops, get dressed and make yourself look presentable enough, it's out the door and off to school. Despite it being school, a place where you spend about six or seven hours concentrating intensely to make sense of the gibberish written on the board, it's actually an okay place to be when your friends are there. They're the only people out there that can actually understand you, and seem to know every weird and wonderful aspect about you too. With them around, you somehow make it through the day.

When the last bell finally rings and you reach home, the sun is shining through the window, the kids are all outside playing, and you're staring at the English essay you've been given to do. Sure, you could have started it in class like everyone else and had the guts of it done, but you and your friend decided that looking out of the window and waving at everyone that walked by was a much better way to spend the afternoon. The blank page stares back at you, and you stare back at it. Suddenly your mind kicks in and offers you some words of wisdom; a three-page essay won't write itself. So you at least attempt it before shoving it at the bottom of your bag. Being the teenager that you are, all this energy that you've used has left you famished, so when dinner comes around, you've got your knife and fork ready.

Alas, when the food comes, you see a sea of green vegetables on your plate. After a few huffs and puffs, quickly silenced by that 'look' from your mother, you just mutter a 'thank you' and eat. The rest of the evening is then left for you to do whatever you want. It usually consists of

    A. Going on the Internet,
        B. Binge watching T.V. or
            C. Actually going outside.

And at the end of the day, you have a hot shower and finally crash on the bed, where the next morning, the entire cycle repeats itself. Unless, that is, you're a night owl and stay up half the night doing something else other than sleeping, and of course, come to regret it in the morning.

In the end though, things like procrastination and staying up late just seem to be normal around this time. Sure, we might change moods every five minutes, have an unnatural physical attachment to our beds or raid the fridge when we're feeling 'peckish' but the beauty if it all is that it's perfectly normal to be this way. Well, at least I hope so, anyways.

MELINDA HUIAN, COUNTY CAVAN, IRELAND

Melinda is just a normal teenager living on the small, rainy island of Ireland, who, like everyone else, enjoys hanging out with friends and having the craic. Apart from that, she loves music and writing and plays piano in her spare time.

The Voice of the Lord

Where there is no prophecy, the people cast off restraint, but happy are those who keep the law.
Proverbs 29: 18 NRSVCE

KATEY MORELAND

INTRODUCTION TO THE VOICE OF THE LORD

When God placed in my heart a plan to publish this anthology, I hardly expected to introduce a section about prophecy! Indeed, the book was almost complete before I had that understanding. A worship leader said she had no songs she could offer for the anthology, but had plenty of prophecies she had recorded. I knew immediately that God planned to include prophecy in this book of collective creative writings. The primary Hebrew word for prophecy is "na*b*a'" (pronounced 'nava'), meaning to speak or sing by inspiration, and to praise God while under divine influence. At first, I thought these divinely inspired words might be integrated amongst the songs and poems, but as I began to set it all in place, I realised prophetic utterances should have their own section.

This anthology is a work of art, each author creativity expressing themselves, together forming a beautiful tapestry. In the same way, we each are a work of God's art, uniquely formed and lovingly appreciated by the Maker. We too form a beautiful tapestry, Christ's Body on the earth, appreciated best from Heaven's viewpoint. I liken the three-part collection within this book to prayer. In sections one and two, adults and young alike have expressed themselves. Prayer, however, is not a one-way monologue, but a two-way relationship between a loving Father and His children. We speak–Our Father in Heaven listens. He speaks–we're *supposed to* listen. Mark Virkler, an American author describes the sound of God's voice as "spontaneous thoughts that light upon your mind". Jesus said He did nothing except He saw the Father do it first (John 5: 19). Throughout the ages, others have followed in Jesus' footsteps. From the time of St. Patrick until now, God has found creative ways to express His heart to the land of Ireland, a people He holds dear. This third section, then, is set out to record God's voice to His children in the land, albeit through imperfect human vessels.

The next anthology (in 2020) will not be so long as it will only have to cover five years of creative writings, whereas, in this one, I attempt to cover seventeen centuries! Please bear with me as we begin with St. Patrick's Confession . . .

My name is Patrick. I am a sinner, a simple country person, and the least of all believers. I am looked down upon by many. My father was Calpornius. He was a deacon; his father was Potitus, a priest, who lived at Bannavem Taburniae. His home was near there, and that is where I was taken prisoner. I was about sixteen. At that time, I did not know the true God. I was taken into captivity in Ireland, along with thousands of others. We deserved this, because we had gone away from God, and did not keep his commandments . . .

It was there that the Lord opened up my awareness of my lack of faith. Even though it came about late, I recognised my failings. So I turned with all my heart to the Lord my God, and he looked down on my lowliness and had mercy on my youthful ignorance. He guarded me before I knew him and before I came to wisdom and could distinguish between good and evil. He protected me and consoled me as a father does his son.

That is why I cannot be silent – nor would it be good to do so – about such great blessings and such a gift that the Lord so kindly bestowed in the land of my captivity. This is how we can repay such blessings, when our lives change and we come to know God, to praise and bear witness to his great wonders before every nation under heaven . . .

After I arrived in Ireland, I tended sheep every day, and I prayed frequently during the day. More and more the love of God increased, and my sense of awe before God. Faith grew, and my spirit was moved, so that in one day I would pray up to one hundred times, and at night perhaps the same . . .

It was there one night in my sleep that I heard a voice saying to me: "You have fasted well. Very soon you will return to your native country." Again after a short while, I heard someone saying to me: "Look – your ship is ready." It was not nearby, but a good two hundred miles away. I had never been to the place, nor did I know anyone there. So I ran away then, and left the man with whom I had been for six years. It was in the strength of God that I went – God who turned the direction of my life to good; I feared nothing while I was on the journey to that ship . . .

Spiritual Songs, Poems and Prophecies

It happened again after many years that I was taken prisoner. On the first night I was with them, I heard a divine answer saying to me: "You will be with them for two months." This is how it was: on the sixtieth night, the Lord freed me from their hands.

A few years later I was again with my parents in Britain. They welcomed me as a son, and they pleaded with me that, after all the many tribulations I had undergone, I should never leave them again. It was while I was there that I saw, in a vision in the night, a man whose name was Victoricus coming as it were from Ireland with so many letters they could not be counted. He gave me one of these, and I read the beginning of the letter, the voice of the Irish people. While I was reading out the beginning of the letter, I thought I heard at that moment the voice of those who were beside the wood of Voclut, near the western sea. They called out as it were with one voice: "We beg you, holy boy, to come and walk again among us." This touched my heart deeply, and I could not read any further; I woke up then. Thanks be to God, after many years the Lord granted them what they were calling for.

Another night– . . .I heard authoritative words which I could hear but not understand, until at the end of the speech it became clear: "The one who gave his life for you, he it is who speaks in you"; and I awoke full of joy.

I am greatly in debt to God. He gave me such great grace, that through me, many people should be born again in God and brought to full life. Also that clerics should be ordained everywhere for this people who have lately come to believe, and who the Lord has taken from the ends of the earth. This is just what he promised in the past through his prophet: "The nations will come to you from the ends of the earth, and they will say: How false are the idols our fathers got for themselves, and they are of no use whatever." And again: "I have put you as a light to the nations, that you may be their salvation to the end of the earth."

It is there that I await his promise – he is the one who never deceives, as is repeated in the gospel: "They will come from the east and from the west, and they will lie down with Abraham and Isaac and Jacob." We believe that believing people will come from all over the world.   St. Patrick's Confession taken from Pádraig McCarthy's translation, Confessio and Epistola English: © 2003

From St. Patrick's Day to the Modern Day

We can see by reading 'St. Patrick's Confession' that after his conversion experience, he lived a life under divine influence, the Lord Jesus directing his path through prophetic dreams and visions. Born about 385 AD, St. Patrick began his ministry in Ireland around 432 AD. For thirty years he zealously continued in the mission God had set for him to convert Ireland to Christianity, even in the midst of hostile and violent responses. The Holy Spirit gave him the ability, not only to understand a foreign tongue but, to testify to the greatness of the One true God in that Gaelic language, bringing thousands into the Kingdom of God through Jesus. He, like so many after him, saw that Ireland is a special land, calling believers to gather here from all over the world.

For a number of centuries after Patrick's death, Ireland thrived as a Christian nation. Multitudes flocked to serve God in monasteries, not exclusively places of prayer, but also hubs of commerce and learning. Patrick's vision for the people of Ireland to be a light to the nations was fulfilled, the Irish zealously serving the Lord in missions to Europe.

St. Bridget of Kildare was part of Patrick's legacy. Born in 451 or 452 AD, Bridget founded a double monastery at Cill-Dara (Kildare) around the year 470 (making her less than 20 years old!). The foundation developed into a centre of learning and spirituality, and around it grew the Cathedral city of Kildare. Bridget also founded a school of art, from which the Book of Kildare, an illuminated manuscript, became famous and claimed much praise before disappearing three centuries ago.

Bridget, like Patrick, had a vision for Ireland far beyond her lifetime. Apparently, in a vision she saw a map of Ireland ablaze with the glory of God. But then the fire died down and Ireland became ashen. She realized this meant that Ireland would enter a 'dark time' but as she cried out to the Lord He said, "Look again." As she did, she saw the fire being rekindled from embers in the north to spread and engulf the whole land, with flames spreading to the north, south, east and west, and she knew, that in the 'last days', the fire of God's love would once again go out from Ireland to the nations. Paul Kyle, a song-writer from Northern Ireland, with reconciliation very much in his heart, was inspired by Bridget's vision to write a song called 'O, Ireland':

PAUL KYLE

O IRELAND

O Ireland,
Emerald isle in crystal sea
O Ireland,
No one bears the mark of Cain like thee
Mountain mist and valley glow
Friendly faces easy go
But from the depths of hell below
A broken heart, a deadly blow

O Ireland,
Fair maid in Eden's sparkling dawn
O Ireland,
Your virgin innocence now gone
You've sold yourself a thousand times
You've paid in blood for all your crimes
And where God's glory might have been,
An empty heart, a shattered dream

O Ireland,
Land of saints and scholars bright
O Ireland,
For your sin you suffer blight
Can no one purge away your shame?
Can no one make you live again?
From heaven's height the answer came–
A bleeding heart, He bore the blame

O Ireland,
From whence the gospel light was shed
O Ireland,
The dove now hovers o'er your head
Only in Jesus could you ever be
One in heart, completely free
And once again, God's love proclaim,
A burning heart in Jesus name
(repeat last 4 lines)

From the 'O Ireland' CD
© Coming King Ministries 1995
www.paulkyle.org

Paul and Hilary Kyle

The darkness Bridget prophesied was to engulf Ireland in what is known as the 'Dark Ages' of Europe. Let us jump to a brighter time when another great pioneer, JOHN WESLEY, followed God's calling to Ireland. Beginning in his mid-forties, Wesley made a total of twenty-one visits over forty-two years (1747-1789), spending five and a half years of his public life in Ireland. Like St. Paul, who was a spiritual father to individuals and whole people groups alike, John Wesley had a father's heart toward the nation of Ireland as well as toward individual Irish believers. In Paul's journeying he found the Bereans more teachable than the Thessalonians (Acts 17: 11) and Wesley likewise noted in his journal that the Irish had more teachable spirits than most of their neighbours in England. He maintained that should he have been given but one (full) year to minister in Ireland, every corner of the nation would have received the truth as it is in Jesus. What could have driven him to ride thousands of miles on horseback around Ireland, setting fires ablaze, even in the midst of persecution, but the Spirit of God spurring him on – here was a land and people chosen by God.

John Wesley had a great effect in his forty-two year ministry, lighting fires all over Ireland, but in 1859 a more incredible thing was to happen. The 'ULSTER REVIVAL' was to see an estimated 100,000 souls swept into the Kingdom of God, all within the space of one year. These were church people whose hearts and minds were revived, through an encounter with the living God. The work of the Holy Spirit was evident in people's lives beyond their intense conviction of sin and crying out for forgiveness, some going into trances and visiting heaven. Oral sources also suggest people spoke in tongues (a language not their own, this can be a language from another country or a heavenly one given by the Holy Spirit, see 1 Corinthians 12). While the Spirit of God was evidently responsible for this transformation, there seems also to have been a restrictive spirit in force. The majority of people to be affected by this move of God were from one group, Scottish Presbyterians living in Ulster. Even though the divide between north and south did not exist then, this visitation of God had little effect on people outside of the six counties. Prophecy also seems to have been restricted. In one account, a minister refused a lay-person the right to share a word from God.[1] Was the young man's heart burning with the knowledge that this was a word in season, a word God wanted the people to receive 'now'? Whatever it was, the lay-person wouldn't give up. In response, the minister cleared the church building. Outside, the young man preached his message from heaven and hundreds not only listened to him, but knelt in the rain and mud, asking God's forgiveness.

Fast forward another hundred years to hear the prophecy allegedly uttered by SMITH WIGGLESWORTH shortly before his death in 1947:

> "During the next few decades there will be two distinct moves of the Holy Spirit across the church in Great Britain. The first move will affect every church that is open to receive it and will be characterized by a restoration of the baptism and gifts of the Holy Spirit. The second move of the Holy Spirit will result in people leaving historic churches and planting new churches. In the duration of each of these moves, the people who are involved will say 'This is the great revival'. But the Lord says "No, neither is this the great revival but both are steps towards it."
>
> "When the new church phase is on the wane, there will be evidenced in the churches something that has not been seen before: a coming together of those with an emphasis on the Word and those with an emphasis on the Spirit. When the Word and the Spirit come together, there will be the biggest movement of the Holy Spirit that the nation, and indeed the world, has ever seen. It will mark the beginning of a revival that will eclipse anything that has been witnessed within these shores, even the Wesleyan and the Welsh revivals of former years. The outpouring of God's Spirit will flow over from the UK to the mainland of Europe, and from there will begin a missionary move to the ends of the earth."

Wigglesworth was speaking about Great Britain, of which Northern Ireland is a part. A similar prophecy was heard for the whole land of Ireland during the 1974 conference held in Limerick of Evangelical believers, Catholics and Protestants, from the North and South of Ireland. SISTER ALPHONSUS, a Catholic nun from Portadown, shared a prophetic picture, portraying, many believe, God's plan and purpose for Ireland. On a map of Ireland, she saw logs were brought from the North to the centre and oil from the South was poured on them. Fire came down from the clouds and set the whole pile ablaze. The fire then swept the length and breadth of Ireland, until the whole land was aflame, spreading to England, Scotland, Wales and Continental Europe.

The interpretation she received from God was the logs represented Evangelical Protestants, steeped in the Word of God from knee high, but who, without the baptism of the Holy Spirit, could become hard and legalistic. The oil represented the Roman Catholics, baptised in the Holy Spirit, full of zeal for God, but lacking foundation in the Word of God. As God would bring the two together, Holy Spirit revival would sweep Ireland, and Ireland would once again become a light to the nations.[2]

BRENDA VANWINKLE

A SONG OF IRELAND

Water from an ancient well
      Percolating
           Bubbling.
Refusing to be still another moment
      One more day.
Reaching, longing, arching upward
    toward the surface,
        Toward the sun.

Too long lay the well, untapped!
Too long lay the spring, unsprung!
A rushing, gushing, vibrating
   river of energy, life
  all that is real and true.
So long lay
        Still.
        Quiet.
        Unmoving.
Breath held. Heart stilled.
        Repose.

And on the surface the face of time passes
   and passes by, again.
Never a question, not a thought to wonder –
  Does this water yet live?

Hope loses her luster in the day.

Until.
The Day.

Second Adam's son awakens from
        his slumber
And with his awakening –
Remembrance.
Those sons of God
        compose a Bride.

Lovely, Complete. Longing.
To dance.

Feet of daughters hands of sons
        dance and clap
           to awaken
                to praise.

Sleepy, unsure voices become strong
        in joy
            and unequaled in all
    of creation.
                in praise.

Delighting in the Bridegroom,
    the vibrations of their
passion for The Name
            begins a stirring.
        A shaking.
An awakening
        in high heaven
and
        in deepest earth.

The expanse of water first separated
        on day two
Become one once again in the
        Third day

        as heaven touches earth
and
        deep calls to deep
as
            waterspouts form.

And the rivers sing.
    The wells erupt.
As those formed of earth
        and water
    in the image of
One
release unity,
        wholeness
         movement
creation

once again.

And it is good.

        Written by Brenda VanWinkle
        January 9, 2013
        Redding, CA
        While interceding for Ireland
        Isaiah 49:8

(American-English spellings left in place)

A year after the conference in Limerick, in May 1975, a number of Irish Charismatic Catholics formed part of a group of 30,000, congregating at St. Peter's Basilica, Rome, for the First International Congress of the Catholic Charismatic Renewal. They speak of being riveted on Pentecost Monday, when two men, RALPH MARTIN and BRUCE YOCUM, gave the following prophecy. It was not an easy word to receive – tribulation and darkness awaiting God's people, but through it all He promised to form an army, a people comforted by the Holy Spirit, and ultimately Christ's glory would shine. Returning home to Ireland with that word planted in their hearts, they have chosen to trust God in a season of stripping both in the Church and society, knowing that, even when persecution increases, Christ Kingdom will prevail. He is all victorious and strengthens his Bride:

> Since I love you, I want to show you what I am doing in the world today. I want you to be prepared for what is to come. Days of darkness are coming for the world, days of tribulation. Buildings that are firm now will stand no more. I want you to be prepared, My people, that you may know Me. I want you who are faithful to Me to know Me in a deeper way than you have in the past. I will lead you into the desert. In that hour I will strip you of all that you depend on now so that you will depend only on Me. A time of confusion is coming on the world, but a time of glory is arriving for My church, a time of glory is coming for My people. Once again I will pour out on you all the gifts of My Spirit. I will prepare you for spiritual combat; I will prepare you for a time of evangelization that the world has never seen. And you won't have anything other than Me, but then you will have all: earth, fields, houses, brothers and sisters, love, joy, peace, even more than you had at first. Be ready My people. I am preparing you. *(Given by Ralph Martin)*

> My people, I speak of the dawn of a new age for My Church. I speak about a day that you have not yet seen. Prepare for the action that I begin now, because the circumstances you see around you they will change. The struggle that you will engage in is new. There is a wisdom, My wisdom, that you need but do not yet have. My holy people, you need the Spirit in a manner that you never have possessed. You need to understand My will, the way in which I operate, which is still unknown to you. Open your eyes! Open your hearts! Prepare for the day that I

begin now. My Church will be different, My people will be different.

Trials and tribulations will come to you. The consolation that you know now will be removed, but the comfort that you will have is the consolation of My Holy Spirit. I will support you. Come to Me. Gather together around Me, in close unity. Prepare, since I proclaim a new day, a day of victory and of triumph for your God. It has started already. *(Given by Bruce Yocum)*

I will renew My people. I make My people into a unified people. I call upon you to leave the pleasures of the world. I call upon you to renounce worldly desires. I call upon you not to look for the approval of the world. I want to transform your life. I have a word for My Church. I am renewing My call. I am raising up a great army. My power will be upon it. It will be led by the shepherds that I have chosen. I am renewing My Church. I will free the world. In these days I want you to know the truth, the truth of My reign, My reign that prevails. I want you to cling to this truth, to abide in the truth, and to believe in the truth. Don't jeopardize it; don't lose it in the confusion, but stand firm. Love with simplicity." *(Given by Ralph Martin)* [3]

God will unite His people, but we have our part to play as well. How must we behave? In the 1980s, the Lord spoke very clearly to Irish writer and international speaker, FR. PAT COLLINS, as he travelled by train to a prayer meeting in America,

> Leave the city with its proud flags and go to the breach in the wall. Go and stand in the breach the place of insecurity. Stand in the breach where the wind blows, where the jackal cries and where the enemy enters under the cloak of darkness. Stand in the breach and listen to my word. Stand in the breach and pray for yourself and the people. Then call My people to the breach to rebuild the walls of Jerusalem.

Fr. Pat shares, "I wasn't sure if these words were from the Lord or not. Following some prayer for help I decided, rightly or wrongly, to cut the bible. If my finger was on the words, 'Rebuild the walls of Jerusalem', I would see them as confirmation of the divine source of my inspiration. I closed my eyes, opened the bible at random. When I looked down, I saw that my finger was on verse 18 of psalm 50, which reads, 'rebuild the walls of Jerusalem'."

In another twenty years God would build on those words. Preparing to preach, Fr. Pat would hear words within himself, so clear and memorable that he was able to write them down:

> I am the Lord your God the holy one. My people, do not compromise with sin. If there is serious sin in your life, do not deny or excuse it. Repent, receive my forgiveness, avoid the first stirrings of temptation and believe that I will deliver you from the web of evil that holds you captive. If there is venial sin in your life, do not tolerate it. Be aware that secret and unrepented sin in the lives of those who believe in me is the greatest single obstacle to the work of my Spirit.
>
> I want you to be holy; I want you to turn away from the ways of the world. I call on you to root out your sins, great and small alike. Be assured that I will not only enlighten your heart to know your sins. I will enable you to turn away from them by a great and liberating outpouring of my grace. Be holy as I am holy. There is no substitute for this holiness. There is no plan, effort, or activity, no matter how well intentioned, which will accomplish my purposes if you are not holy like Me. When your heart is cleansed, my Spirit will pray ardently within you, it will guide you in ways you have not known, it will empower and protect you from the deceptions of the evil one. It will fill you with my joy.
>
> I weep for the world and my Church. There are many, who because of their great and repeated sins are travelling the wide road that leads to perdition. Call them to repentance, before it is too late, so that they may come back to me. I promise you that many of them will heed your words when they see my holiness shining forth in your lives. My people, the time of breach-mending is at hand. I will enable you to re-build the walls of Jerusalem. I am about to accomplish a great work of restoration, but woe to those who do not heed my voice.

SAMUEL B OGILBY received a word from God on the same theme of re-building the walls of Jerusalem. Born in Carrickfergus in 1945, he lived and worked in London for 40 years, and was a member of Holford House Christian Fellowship under the leadership of well known messianic pastor, teacher and author, Lance Lambert. Returning to N. Ireland in 2001, he received a prophecy from the Lord in 2003:

> Little Ireland, you have a special place in my heart. Just like little Israel, great things have come forth from you. It was from

Israel that I sent forth My Beloved Son to be your Saviour. It was from you that I sent forth my word across Europe, yes, and even to the uttermost parts of the earth. I delight to take that which is small and make it great. It is for that very reason that I will pour out the greatest measure of My glory in these last days on little Israel and little Ireland. You are as twin children to me, and I have chosen you, little Ireland, to be a dwelling place for My glory. My enemy knows just how important you are to me, and has brought many sorrows on you. Just as My people Israel were scattered to the four corners of the earth, so were you. But I am now gathering you back together again in preparation for those things which must come to pass before My Son returns to take up His rightful place as your King. My children, do not grow weary in waiting for Me, for I will come to you at the appointed time, and your patience will be fully rewarded. So lift up your heads, because My glory is about to fall on you, and you will see things greater than your wildest dreams. I am your Father and I love you beyond measure.

Holy Spirit also spoke about God's heart toward Ireland through a Messianic Jew, W. ARIEL KEREN OR, from Israel on January 17th 2007, while he visited the Ring of Kerry, as part of his ministry in Ireland:

Ireland is a divided family and my heart is bleeding for this nation, but I, I alone will unify them and I will bring them altogether in the palm of my hands! How many of you are really willing to save and to love the lost souls ten thousand times more than you love yourselves and your own ministries? When someone thinks about unity, he is planning how he would bring my people under his controlling spirit. Your differences must complete and not divide each other. Because in your unity I will give power and authority to fight the evil, and in your obedience I will bless you' says Jehovah of Hosts.

The Lord has spoken to His children about the problem of disunity for decades, not only giving national words, but local ones. The following poem is a prophecy Jesus gave to Roger Skillington in 1988, 'a word for Cork' but it could have just as easily been a word to any town in Ireland. In fact, it may have been duplicated – a different vessel, a different location, but the Lord voicing the same problem that grieves His heart so much. "Unless My people unite", He declares, "they will not see the revival for which they pray".

ROGER SKILLINGTON

WORD FOR CORK

You are one in Jesus.
Nothing can pull you apart.
No building or name can divide you,
For in Jesus all are one.

There is one way to God: Jesus;
One path to heaven through Him.
There is one forgiveness in Jesus.
One cleansing through His blood.

So how can you stay apart,
Going along your own roads.
Sitting alone in your buildings.
Interpreting My word your own ways?

My body you've broken and divided,
Fragmented into pieces so small.
Come let My hands and My feet come together,
Combining once again with my trunk.
When you are one, I'll again be the Head.

My body in Cork is divided,
Crucified once again by you,
For you've torn My body asunder
And labelled each part as your own.
My body's been scourged once again
By your gossiping backbiting tongues.
My wounds you have opened up wider,
With your brads of hatred and fear.
Come walk in love as I have loved and died for you.

So repent of this evil among you,
And come for forgiveness to Me.
So get out of your boxes My children,
And come together in My harmony.
For My hands need My feet and Mine eyes.
My voice needs Mine ears to be heard.
When you are one, the power of My Spirit
Will win many in your city for Me,
And My glory will shine forth through you.

So remember you're one in Jesus.
Nothing can pull you apart.
No building or name can divide you,
For in Jesus all are one.
There is one way to God: Jesus;
There is one way to heaven through Him.
There is one forgiveness in Jesus.
One cleansing through His blood.

On inviting Jesus into his life in 1977, Roger felt completely changed internally. Since then he has received poetry from the Lord, including the word (written above) for Cork which he received in 1988. Roger shares, "I went to my pastor, Mike O'Brien to show it to him but he was not available as he was in the library writing out his sermon for the next Sunday. When he had finished, he read the word I had got and was amazed as he had just written on the same theme for his sermon."

As we entered the twenty-first century, Christians all over the land could be heard asking, "Will this be the time? Will the fires deep within the ancestry of our land burn once again? Will we see revival?" Certainly, in this century, God has spoken through many international intercessors, declaring through them that Ireland will be much more than we can even hope for. On February 15th 2000, DOMINIQUE FRANCOIS wrote encouragingly to Ireland, from Paris, France:

IRELAND! PUT ON THE GARMENTS OF PRAISE!
Although I have been a born again Christian for 30 years and in this prophetic renewal for many, I have never ever received a vision and a word like the one God seized me with for Ireland this morning.

As I was listening to the song 'O, consuming fire', I saw the map of Europe circled by a high and thick wall, like a fortified city. Coming from the sea, I saw the stem of a big ship - (icebreaker-type thing) only much bigger, knocking this wall down and making a breakthrough in Europe through Ireland. I said: "God, are you going to bring a revival or a renewal to Ireland?" He answered: "No. Revival or renewal are not adequate words for what I am about to do in this country. It is going to be an outburst, an explosion, an invasion of my Spirit in the land of Ireland. All they have known for decades is civil war, terrorism, bombs, bullets, explosions, slaughters which were the works of the enemy because satan knows what an exceptional destiny I have for the Irish people, but now I come, I come with might and power, I come with glory and splendour, I come with a divine explosion."

Then the Lord led me to listen to the first song of "REVIVAL IN BELFAST" (Hosanna Music) and the sobs of the Father's heart for Ireland seized me with violence. The lyrics say:
"PUT ON THE GARMENTS OF PRAISE FOR THE SPIRIT OF HEAVINESS. LET THE OIL OF GLADNESS FLOW DOWN FROM YOUR THRONE."

Ireland, REJOICE! The Lord of glory is coming to you in an unprecedented explosion of his manifest presence and all of Europe will be impacted and in awe of what the God has done for you.

"When the Lord brought back the captive ones of Zion, we were like those who dream. Then our mouth was filled with laughter and our tongue with joyful shouting. Then they said among the nations, the Lord has done great things for them, the Lord has done great things for us, we are glad." (Psalm 126)

May this word stir up your hearts, renew your courage and hope and enlarge your vision. We cannot fathom what God is about to do.

In his wonderful love,

Ms Dominique Francois, Paris, France [4]

In this present century, God not only shared his intentions for Ireland with international intercessors, but made declarations to individuals within the country about groups they did not belong to. In Fr. Pat Collins' book, 'He Has Anointed Me', he records a word that a Church of Ireland clergyman, REV DON GAMBLE, spoke on 7th February 2003, during a time of intercession in Belfast. He notes, "In view of their origin, they are as surprising as they are encouraging. Part of the prophetic message reads:

> The Lord has been shaking the Roman Catholic Church. He holds the church in the palm of His hand and he has been shaking it for 20 to 25 years. The church has been rattling around like a nut in a nutshell. All the time the Lord has been shaking it from the outside. Now He is going to work on the inside. He throws the church down and cracks it open. A holy and pure church is exposed, what was hidden before can now be seen. As the church, broken, flows out, the Glory of God flows in, like a river of liquid gold. This is how the Lord is going to work in the church. Everything in the church that has only been experienced in symbolism and token will now be experienced in full *(Eph 1: 13-14)*.
>
> The candle light – is the Light of Christ,
>
> the incense – is the fragrance of Jesus,
>
> the wafer bread – is the Body of Christ,
>
> the honoring of saints and angels – is holiness and visitations. Could it be that symbolism has sustained the church between revivals and kept God's pilot light burning. Soon this generation who have known only symbolism will experience the reality of God *(1 Cor. 13:12)*. This will spread through the Catholic Church infrastructure worldwide, producing great love and devotion for the Lord."[5]

Some of you are wondering whether it's true that God speaks to people, let alone, if these words can be true. Throughout the Bible God spoke to people and we've seen God gave Saints Patrick and Bridget, spiritual parents of Ireland, visions to tell them of their own future and the future of our land. Lynne Mary-Lou has written a poem this century, referring to events that happened last century, that confirm to her that God speaks – and we should listen:

GOD SPEAKS

LYNNE MARY-LOU

Why is it when we talk to God
Then that is called prayer?
Yet when God speaks to us
Then that is called crazy?
God Speaks
Yes that's right, God speaks
Just because we are too busy talking
And not tuned in to listen
Doesn't mean that God is mute
God Speaks
Go!!! Get out of that night club now
He Says
Before any evidence of trouble
Exiting the door and glancing back
Pint glasses go hurling through the air
Yes God Speaks.
Awake and get up... there's a deadly leak
Take your family back home
Returning home safely
We learn that Sellafield let loose its nuclear waste
Saved from contamination and radiation
Praise God for He does speak
Just after visiting the Berlin wall and East Berlin
Whilst still in East Germany
God Spoke
GO! GO! GO! Explosions. Quickly, GO!
We were gone
Through the German corridors
Back into West Germany
Soon after we saw the sky light up like a burning sunset
Six British soldiers died in that bomb attack
Yet God spoke and saved my friend, my almost three year old
And my baby seven months gestation
And to go without saying
Me of course
Why did we live . . . and why did they die?
I cannot answer
All I know is
God Speaks
No it is not crazy when God speaks to you
However it is crazy to not listen!

OLIVIA RALPH wrote the following poem on her birthday, 8th July 2005 at 3pm, in a park in Mitchelstown, Co. Cork. She was merely passing through. The day before London had been bombed and many people were killed and injured. At the time Olivia was experiencing a great difficulty in her own life. She poured out her heart to the Lord and received Psalm 69:1-3 in her spirit. The poem 'Moments' flowed from there.

OLIVIA RALPH

MOMENTS

I've seen all your moments from the moment I conceived you
in your mother's womb.
I saw your identity, I saw your potential,
I saw your vastness, your creativity.
Your beauty within, I hold deep within my own beauty.

I am your creator, your lover,
you are My love.
I have loved you with an everlasting love,
I have drawn you with an everlasting kindness,
My kindness is unconditional,
I don't expect anything in return.
Draw near and you will know your lover, your creator.

How much I want to celebrate your presence,
I want to be with you.
I've created your presence, I want to enjoy it with you.
I am the great "I AM",
I AM present to My own presence
and I want you to enjoy your presence,
for this is My creation.

I want to enjoy your presence.
How important you are to Me, how I want you to experience
My closeness and Intimacy.
In this you will experience closeness and intimacy for yourself
and for others.
Draw close to My love, draw close.

CATHERINE BROWN, Founder/Director of Gatekeepers Global Ministries and Co-founder of Scottish Apostolic Networking Enterprise, shares, "On July 3rd 2010, whilst in prayer for a trip to Ennis, Southern Ireland, the Holy Spirit began to speak sweet and powerful words about this blessed land:

THE SONG OF HEAVEN OVER IRELAND

'Ireland has a song; the song is buried deep in the heart of Ireland; the heart of Ireland is buried deep in the people; and the people are buried deep in pain. But the Father has a song that He is singing over Ireland. And the Bridegroom has a song that He is singing over Ireland. And the Holy Spirit has a wind that He is breathing over Ireland.

'It is a holy wind;
It's a healing wind;
It's a wind of harmony;
It's a wind of unity,
It's a wind of peace.'

THE DRUM, THE DANCE AND THE FATHER'S HEARTBEAT

Into this heavenly declaration unfolding in my spiritual hearing, God poured out imagery and further sounds. I heard the beat of an unstoppable drum as a crescendo that was being poured out from Heaven and released to earth. With an almost involuntary response, I was almost unable to prevent myself from responding, and my gladly feet began to tap to the tune of the Father's heartbeat over Ireland.

With this, a powerful scene unfolded before my eyes – an army of traditional Irish dancers, anointed for spiritual warfare, who danced to the tune of a sound that originated in Heaven. Their feet were anointed to bring the Good News of Jesus Christ. My physical being felt waves of anointing flowing from the throne of God as I witnessed this wonderful prophetic scene and prayed for revival in Ireland.

The Holy Spirit began to speak again, and my ears filled up with harmonies ancient and new, with the sounds of the drums, the pipes and the timbrels:

'There is an ancient song: ancient melodies with the new wine that is being poured out for Ireland. There is a drum and an army of drummers who will march to the standard of the King of Heaven. There are pipers to whom the Holy Spirit will give breath and stamina for worship rallies and parades upon the streets of Ireland.

'A new wave of public worship is rising up from the earth of Ireland, a wave of worship that has no secular connotations, but reverberates with the holy passion of our Heavenly Father. A passion for souls, a passion for righteousness, a passion for discipleship. Ireland, arise from the ashes of a crushed generation and sing a new song to the nations, sing a new a song and dance a new dance for the glory of your Father.'

The parade of worshippers continued to be added to as melody was laid upon melody and harmony upon harmony, creating a breakthrough sound in Heaven and on earth. To the dancers came those with timbrels adorned with ribbons, and they whirled around in adoration to the King.

AFRICAN CO-LABOURERS ARISE IN IRELAND

To the parade of worshippers there now came African brothers and sisters. I saw many Africans praying, and they joined the Irish song and dance-led worshippers in a divinely created alliance, and I heard the Holy Spirit say:

'This is an example of a cross-continental, collaborative strategy. I am calling forth an anointed army of warrior worshippers that know how to pray and know how to worship, but it will take the coming together of two continents in Ireland to produce the breakthrough anointing that I desire to pour out upon Ireland.'

The final words of the Holy Spirit that I heard were, 'There is a breakthrough anointing upon the dance and a breakthrough anointing upon the song.'
To God be all glory! *Catherine Brown*"[6]

© Masha Duna

Below is a transcription of a prophetic song for the Body of Christ received by a home-grown prophetic worship leader, CAROL MAHON, in February 2012–Words, once again telling us of God's love, His desire for personal intimacy, and cummunal unity weighing heavily upon His heart:

Whereas before you've longed to see Me, today, in this season of your life, you *will* see Me, oh so clearly as never before, not just in a dream or vision. But I want to reveal Myself to you, My children, and I'm extending My hand. Reach out, reach out, and take My hand today and look into My face, the face of your brother, the face of your saviour and your friend. And you'll see Me so much clearer; you'll see My beauty as never before. Before it was a dim reflection or a thought of what you thought I looked like. But in this season of your lives, My children, I want you to see Me as I truly am; I want you to experience Me as I am.

So reach out and take My hand and look into My eyes and see My face and experience who I truly am and not a dim reflection of your imagination–I am here. I stand before you. I'm reaching out My hand to you today. Look up and see Me standing before you and take hold of My hand. And I shall pull you up to My breast and I shall wrap you in My warmth and My embrace and I'll take you into a dance with Me, just you and I, just you and I–a waltz of love, a waltz of passion, a waltz of romance . . . Let Me take you in My hands, let's dance. I want to hold you so tight. I want you to feel My embrace. I want you to see My eye for you and My mouth as it smiles. I want you to feel My kisses on your lips. I want you to feel My embrace, so strong, yet so gentle. This is how we shall go along together. This is how I'm drawing My bride to My side. My bride, her identity in Me–in Me, not in her plans, not in what she perceives is Me, not in vanities or false identities, but in Me.

Will you let Me dance with you and show you the new dance . . . a new dance, it's a new dance . . . it's a new love dance; it's a new love romance for this season, for this age. As you and I–together, as one, and I with My bride, romancing her in My arms . . . that is where she'll find her true identity. Can you do anything apart from Me? Can you go far on your own without collapsing of exhaustion? No, you were meant to go with Me together. And you'll find a new ease, and new keys in your life. And you'll find a coming together with those where unity has escaped one another. And one will lay down their life for another. And one will lift another up in honour and My glory and when My bride is walking in this way, I am here, I am here. It shall be so attractive to those who are still trying to dance on their own; it shall be a magnetic pull and they shall wonder is 'there a place for Me'? But I'll draw them in, yes I'll draw them in and together they shall find a place in My heart. And even though there are many streams; even though there's many expressions of Me upon the face of this earth, those who will fly and those who will know Me will all have the same dance of love and intimacy. This shall be a mark of authenticity.

Then this is one way that you will know My true bride and this is a way you shall know where I truly live. And this is a way you shall protect yourself against the false and wolves that would try to hide, because without Me, it is not possible, without Me, it is not possible to live in this way, and the wolves will be exposed because they shall boast with pride and arrogance and say 'look at Me – look at what I have done, look at what I have accomplished for the kingdom', but it shall be like a gonging bell, it shall be like a discord within you; even though it may be delivered with a smooth and slick tongue.

And I want you to teach and lead by example those around you and teach what I have told you and what I have put inside of you. So let us dance together as one. Take My hand and let Me draw you close to My bosom. Dance with Me and feel My heartbeat. That is where you will know My voice and My truth.

In March 2012, Carol once again received a word for believers in Ireland as she sang in worship:

> Let go of the life ring, let go of the boat you're clinging on to, let go of all you know, let go, let go, let go, let go, let go . . . Can you see Jesus calling out to you? Whether you want to swim or whether you want to walk over to Him, He's there, He's calling you away . . . will you let go of all security, of all that you would hold on to? This is the adventure of a lifetime, this offer is to you.
>
> Come, come, come, come, My son. Come, come, come, come, My daughter. Look at Me, look at Me, look at Me . . . not

at your circumstances . . . do you trust Me by now? Surely, you trust Me by now . . .

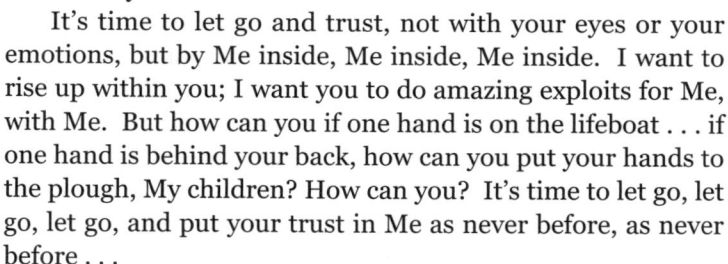

It's time to let go and trust, not with your eyes or your emotions, but by Me inside, Me inside, Me inside. I want to rise up within you; I want you to do amazing exploits for Me, with Me. But how can you if one hand is on the lifeboat . . . if one hand is behind your back, how can you put your hands to the plough, My children? How can you? It's time to let go, let go, let go, and put your trust in Me as never before, as never before . . .

Will you trust in My word, or will you trust in what you have heard? Because he has deceived you, time, time, time, time and again. You have been given some wisdom from many people, but it is time to make up your own mind, make up your own mind, and follow Me. Will you follow Me? It's not just ticking a box saying "yes" to Me, it's so much more than that, My children, children, children. Will you let go of all things? Come, take off your lifejacket too, you will not be needing that because I'm calling you down to the deep, deep, deep oceans, the deep, deep seas of revelation, where the hidden, hidden treasures are. How can you dive down deep with a lifejacket on your back? . . .

There was a flurry of excitement in Ireland in January 2013 as a prophetic word given by CHUCK PIERCE circulated Ireland–by email, by word of mouth, by photocopies, the word flew rapidly in every direction. Chuck's own ministry focuses on prophecy, while much of his activity focuses on supporting other ministries in the apostolic movement (those seeking to restore to the church, elements of the five-fold ministry described in the letter to the Ephesians [chapter 4, verses 11-16]). Whilst teaching in Dublin, on 22nd January 2013, at an event hosted by Rhema Restoration Ministries from Northern Ireland, Chuck received a word for the land of Ireland. LINDA CHRYSTAL took on the difficult task of transcribing Chuck's word to Ireland which came at different times during a teaching session. Her transcription (with narration is in brackets) reads:

> God speaks from Heaven, "Behold I stand over the door of Ireland and I knock, for I say that deposited within the ground and the atmosphere is a dimension of 'First Love' that no other nation has known other than my land of Israel. And I say to you that you have not lost your first love, but tonight a new

knocking begins and I will open the doors over you these next 2 years and my first love, that has grown dormant, will begin to rise again, and out of this love there will be a faith explosion that goes from–(and this is what the door looks like)–I will bring a faith explosion from the South East to North East. Then I will spread West. I say here in the centre of this nation, I will erect a pole that causes a tent of glory to arise, and not only will my knocking be heard, but my entrance will be heard of . . . I say, it will be known that Ireland has opened the door to my glory and my passion to come again."

There is a 'Now' dimension over Ireland this year. We have always prophesied from Northern Ireland, but this year there is a 'Now' dimension over Ireland. This is what I saw when I heard that sound and that knocking going on–all of sudden I saw a door from South East Ireland. I don't know where that is and I don't know what's there or what city is there, but all of a sudden, a door from Heaven opened up and a wind stirred up over South East Ireland. A wind came down from Heaven and began to stir up. There will be a storm as a sign coming from that direction. Watch for it, I mean a tremendous and unusual storm.

Then I saw North East and I think, with God's heart, Northern Ireland – Ireland . . . Its LAND, I saw North East, I'm not sure what that is, the furthest point of North East of this Island and I don't know where that is. I saw another wind come forth. Now here's your sign for it–you have to watch for signs, people, or else you miss how you're being pointed to the future. And this wind came from the North, an unusual wind, and unusual wind from the South and all of a sudden, in the Centre of Ireland, a glory shaft came down.

(Chuck turns and asked Sheila "where are we?" and she replies, "we're in the East and we're more central".)

Now I see this glory shaft being created. Now, this is what began to happen . . . It was during the spring and she began to have babies prematurely, but this is what began to happen– conceptions that could not occur prior to now, the air was impregnated and all of a sudden, conceptions starting happening all over Ireland. I mean physical conceptions. People started conceiving the next generation–it wasn't just spiritual, it was physical as well, things began to happen. You'll hear of people getting pregnant around April, during that time

March to May when they have not been able to get pregnant before. You'll start hearing of things happening, you know why? Because God's coming in from Heaven, there's a door coming open . . . now granted, the husband and wife are going to have to work with the Lord; it's not an immaculate conception or anything like that! All of a sudden, new births are signs!

Now there is going to be incredible linking from South to North. I saw it differently than I've ever seen it before because I could only say from the North you needed to network, but it's this incredible linking that's going to start occurring and then there's this wind that moved west, which is sort of unusual and it moved west across the Island and it was spiritual and all these places began to connect and all these things began to happen. And I don't know how to explain this, but a power of captivity that was over Ireland began to shatter. Let's thank God for the shattered captivity that's coming."
(Prophetic teaching begins, and Chuck jumps in and out of teaching and prophetic words throughout the whole evening.)
I hear the Lord saying something right now . . . He's saying, "Even though the economy of Ireland is fragile, I say to you, it will be known that in the midst of changes, Ireland will be one of the nations that is determining how supply lines will go in the days ahead. I say, you will be sought after as a centre to develop supply storage and supply houses in days ahead." So see, it's an intercessory year, we've got to fill this gap in from the past season, we've got to move so the gap is filled in.

Now here's the thing I want to say to you, of all the years you've known, you might be 70 years old, or who out there is 73? You might have seen and heard things, going around the mountain before. Don't go around the mountain this year. If you're 30, don't go around the mountain this year. If you're 45, don't go around the mountain again this year because this year we have to go up, we can't go around, we cross a bridge and we move up. We have to keep moving this year. What's been desolate has been ok . . . you've continued to build and worship in the midst of changing times, but this year something happens! And see you don't go around because if you go around, you're going to get in a rut and you're going to get stuck and you'll be stuck for 7 years . . . And this is for this nation, I hear this—vision will start ebbing away, and you know what the word 'vision' is—prophetic utterance. Without vision, without prophetic utterance, people go backwards. You don't want to do that, but see you go UP! And before long, you're above all the clouds that clouded your vision in past seasons, and who in here hasn't had times when it got cloudy and said, "It's just easier to stop".

Song of Songs 4 talks about 'going up', Deuteronomy talks about going up and Revelation 4 talks about 'Come up here'.

Ireland is known.... but Ireland will be known!

The Lord spoke to me. He said Ireland will become his threshing floor now because you will become his threshing floor. That is an incredible promise: to see what is about to happen in this nation. Genesis 22 – First Threshing Floor – Abraham – Provision. A new dimension of provision because God came, Jehovah Jireh, the one who can show you your provision for the future.

(Chuck teaches on the importance of the sounds of worship and praise and clapping, even when we don't want to and how this is a key strategy for breakthrough in this land.)

Now I believe this is why God brought me here this year—to say He knows your past. He knows the promises that have been released, and many leaders have come attempting to activate those promises, but that's not what this year is about. This year is about bridging what has been, so the next piece of your future for your children and your children's children begins to blossom. This is the year that the next portion is unlocked.

So what God asked me to do was to carry seven of these mantles to new places and decree, "This is your year for the new identity of God and the next dimension of God to be activated". Abraham was old. He had tremendous promises, BUT GOD! He began to speak out of worship, so that the next generation could advance into a fullness of everything he longed to do.

And why do I feel we needed to be in Dublin? I don't come because other people said I should come. I come because God says, "I must have a representative to decree what Heaven wants, so that My people can be encourage to move into the fullness of it". And why He said come to Dublin was because this is where the tent peg, the centre of the move of God starts permeating. There's a stirring from the South, there's a great movement that comes from the North, but here in the Centre

is where the Lord is ready to bring his glory in, in a new way. *(Pastors and prophetic ministries leaders come and take each end of the mantle and the mantle was lifted up.)*
Remember the lady who pressed through and touched Jesus' garment and was healed. We're going to lift this up and decree, "This is the beginning of the change of atmosphere all across Ireland. This is the beginning for God to unlock New dimensions of prophetic destiny" . . .

(Continues prophesying) And I say to you this mantle will go from South to North, this mantle will cover across to the West, and Ireland will once again come alive to My purposes. I say to you, if you will move in what I am decreeing, provision, supernaturally will be unlocked for the future of Ireland . . . I will unlock creative ways in Ireland that all the world will say, "that idea came from Ireland". I say to you, this is the beginning of a new identity where I bridge the past and I unlock the future of this land.

(Chuck prays) Father we say right now, the lock that holds the past in place and keeps us from moving forward, we command that lock to fall apart and to come open across Ireland. We set a bloodline from South to North and we say the enemies will not be able to move . . .

(Chuck returns to prophesying) And I say to you, the South will try to rise up against the move of God and the North will try to create confusion, but I say to you, there is a move of my Spirit that is moving in this land that now will be fathered and mothered in a new way. I say to you, Get Ready, for the old will rejoice and scream, and the young will dance and shout! I say to you, A New Move Now is being lifted across this land. Some of you have prodigals that the Lord is starting to call back. Over the last three years He's been calling them . . . This year they start saying, "I'm hearing the Lord, I'm hearing the Lord!" They're returning. I say, the sons and the daughters that carry the prophetic anointing for the future are returning again to the worship of the house of God.

(Mantle is placed across the pulpit) . . . and we are going to decree that the pulpits of all of Ireland will awaken to the new mantle that's flowing from Heaven across this land.

Let's worship, let's worship Him.[7]

A worshipper in Ireland, who chooses to remain anonymous, was originally given the song below in 2013, for a person with an eating disorder, yet it also was penned to encourage people in their walk when they are facing 'giants in the land', as fear distorts and disorientates who they are and where they are going. Scripture encourages us to make melody in our hearts with Spirit-led words, words that have the ability to change the atmosphere and strengthen us for the road ahead. Hence the recurring refrain from the LORD, "Fear not for I am with you wherever you go!" The author invites you to make up your own melody. "Better still", he suggests, "ask the Holy Spirit to give you a new song. You will be surprised as you worship in Spirit and truth."

ANONYMOUS

BLESSINGS

Let Your peace rise, Your peace rise,
Your peace rise deep from within my all
Let Your peace rise, Your precious peace rise,
Your peace rise deep from within my all

Fear not
For I am with you
Wherever you go

Let Your glory fall, Your glory fall,
Your glory fall all around me, Lord
Let Your glory fall, Your great glory fall,
Your glory fall all around me, Lord

Fear not
For I am with you
Wherever you go

Let Your praise flow, Your praise flow,
Your praise flow from the bottom of my heart
Let Your light shine, Your light shine,
Your light shine all around me, Lord

Fear not
For I am with you
Wherever you go

Let Your hope live, eternal hope live,
Your hope live through the heavens in my heart
Let Your glory fall, Let your glory fall,
Your glory fall from the heavens round my home

Fear not
For I am with you
Wherever you go

Let Your water wash, Your living water,
Your water wash me pure as the driven snow
Let Your presence rest, Your presence rest,
Your presence rest on the ground whereon I walk

Fear not
For I am with you
Wherever you go

Let Your angels be a company,
A company of comfort as I go
Let Your Spirit guide, Your Holy Spirit
Guide my path, whether high or low

Fear not
For I am with you
Wherever you go

> *. . . fear not, for I am with you and will bless you . . .*
> *Gen 26: 24 (RSCVE)*

Carol Mahon, whose prophecies were recorded in earlier pages, has transcribed hundreds of words given by the Lord in worship. I choose the one below, a message from heaven given through DENIS DOWLING during a time of prophetic worship in September 2013, because it reveals God's desire for His children to be like Him:

> "Won't you be holy for me, even as I am the Holy One?
> Would you walk a holy walk for me?
> Will you be my town crier? Will you walk your town for me?
> Will you walk a holy walk for me?
> Will you catch the sounds of heaven? Will you catch the sounds from heaven?
> Will you bind and loose from heaven?
> Will you speak words in your townland for me – words that are sent from heaven?
> Will you throw the seed as you walk? Will you walk a holy walk?
> Will you be a holy land? Will you speak the sounds from heaven?
> Will you hear what heaven says?
> Will you speak words of deliverance?
> Will you speak words of redemption?
> Will you speak words of healing?
> Will you speak words of deliverance?
> Will you speak words of glory?
> Will you sing words of mercy?
> Will you speak words of grace?
> Will you speak words of new beginnings?
> Will you speak words that set the captives free?
> Will you speak words that cause the blind to see?
> Will you speak words that usher in my Kingdom", says the Lord?
> "For my anointing is upon you to walk a holy walk for me, to declare that my Kingdom has come to your town, to your family, to your townland, says the Lord.
>
> "So will you walk with me? For I desire to walk with you and take you on my holy walk, a deeper place, that your life be known as the holy land, for the Holy One walks in that place. And you, following in His footsteps, walking a holy walk, ushering in My Kingdom. Hallelujah.
>
> "Let me wash your soles, let me wash your feet; let me

prepare you for the holy walk. Walk with me and see the wonders of the Kingdom. Hear what Heaven speaks, see what Heaven does, sing melodies from my throne. See the coming of your King and see My salvation and see that My Kingdom has come to your townland", says the Lord.

Response from Carol (on behalf of the corporate Body):

Lord, we want to walk in step with you. Lord, we want to walk in a holy place, from Your heart, from that place that you walked. Lord we want to walk in Your steps you've placed before us. Lord we want to walk in Your Holiness, set apartness, a consecrated-ness, separated-ness. So we can bring Your word, so we can bring Your voice, so we can bring Your heart, so we can shower Your mercy, shower Your grace. Lord we want you to go with us, Your presence to go with us, only Your presence. Lord we want to walk in Your Holy ways. Lord we offer our feet for you to wash. Lord we offer our souls for you to wash clean. Cleanse our hearts, cleanse our minds, cleanse our souls and everything within us Lord. Cleanse our eyes, cleanse our ears, cleanse our hands and our feet, cleanse our tongues Lord.

HOLY, HOLY, HOLY IS THE LORD.

A number of people, intercessors especially, hear words or see pictures from God through which He shares what has happened, what is happening and what will happen, both with regards to the work of the Lord and the work of man. SARAH O'NEILL, from her Irish home overlooking the sea, writes a blog, keeping a record of what she sees and hears in the spiritual realm. One reason she does this is she wants to give little snippets and snapshots, a foretaste of what is to come and is already coming, and to let God's word do its work. I share here what Sarah saw and heard from the Lord in November 2013:

WHAT ARE YOU DOING HERE, ELIJAH?
A WORD FOR IRELAND

So here's what I saw, and here's what I heard...
I saw Elijah on Mount Horeb.
And I heard the Lord say to him, "What are you doing here, Elijah?"

Only, Elijah was Ireland...!

What are you doing here, Ireland?
What are you doing in this cave? How did you get here?
It is not I who brought you here!
You are not here by My command, but by your own hand!

WHAT ARE YOU DOING HERE, ELIJAH?

And just as He said to Elijah on that mountain,
He is now saying to Ireland, "GO BACK!"
Go back the way you came.
Go back and find the ancient paths.
Go back and complete your call.

IRELAND, YOU HAVE A CALL!
Come out of the cave! Come out of your place of hiding! Come out of your place of retreat! This is not a time for retreating! This is a time for advancing! Come out and stand in the presence of the Lord!

You have been called. You have been chosen. Leaving the call, abandoning the task is *not* an option - you will only be *sent back*! Go back and find the ancient paths. Go back to the pattern of the early church. Do the things you did at first!

It's time to leave the cave. It's time to complete your God-given task, your assignment, your call - your irrevocable call! Go back and finish what was started. Go and anoint your successor. Go and prepare the next generation.
God says we had our Mount Carmel.
Patrick on the hill was our Mount Carmel.
Fire on the Hill. First Fire.
It's time to get back to work, to finish what was started.

And God says that His fire on the hill, HIS HOLY FIRE, will lick up all unholy fire! That just as the snake from Moses' staff swallowed up all the other snakes, so shall God's holy fire swallow up all the other fires - all unholy fire, all unauthorised fire!

From First Fire to Finishing Fire –
THIS IS THE TIME OF THE FINISHING FIRE!
Now GO! Am I not sending you! It's time![8]

In 2009, Festus Alohan, a Bible school director in Egypt, was instructed with his wife, Amy, to give up their home and ministry in Egypt in order to live in Ireland as intercessors. Since that time, God has shared with Festus and Amy one of His plans for Ireland:

> The Lord revealed to me the Christ Catholic Church being birthed out of the Roman Catholic Church. I saw the revival fire of God coming upon the Catholic Church of Ireland. We have carried these two revelation from the Lord in our spirit for some years now in the place of intercession. What the Lord is about to do in the Catholic Church of Ireland will amazed many!
>
> My wife had a revelatory dream about what the Lord is about to do with the Catholic Church of Ireland. In this dream, the Catholic Church was gathered in one place praying and the Protestant church was also gathering together, praying close to the Catholic gathering. All of a sudden, the Catholic gathering began to lift up and ascend. The Protestant gathering stood in amazement, seeing what was happening to the Catholic gathering. The Lord will amaze his church with what He can do with the despised. The revelation and wonders of God is coming upon the Catholic Church. It is exciting what He is about to do.[9]

Two international speakers gave prophetic words to Ireland exactly one year apart. The first was from Sharon Stone. In October 2013, at a mentoring day in her home town of Windsor, UK, Sharon said:

> In speaking into Ireland, it doesn't take a genius to see that's the Western Gate of revival for the UK. That means that if God is moving from the west eastwards, they're carrying something that those in England have need of. Does that make sense?" *(Sharon draws the attention of intercessors to her points, and then reads from her notes of what she heard)*: This is what the Spirit of God, the Lord says, "You're the Western Gate of revival, so it's crisis time for your heart.
>
> *(Speaks to intercessors)* In the heart of the nation I am bringing a brief shock, like a defibrillator. In the heart of Ireland I am bringing a brief shock to reset the heart rhythm. The reason is because Ireland has always been a 'sending' nation *(i.e. of people all around the world)* but they have benefitted more nations than they've benefitted themselves. It's now time to revive the heart of your nation. Just as man

has cut the nation in half, I will heal the laceration portion with prayers for revival. From the west coast to the east coast on your border scar, I will turn yesterday's violence into an arm of strength, an arm of strength that will hurl My spear of revival."[10]

The second word was from CINDY JACOBS on a visit to Ireland in October 2014:

> The Lord would want you to put shields up for this nation, for the enemy is at your door and wants to come in. We were walking down the street today and I felt such a holy caution that we have to pray and that someone is going to try and do something that will cause damage and create some kind of crisis, and **it doesn't have to happen!** So the Lord says: "Shields up, anoint your shields for battle and prepare the shields", and the Lord says, "Prepare, and I am going to expose, expose, expose . . ."
>
> The Lord says, "There is a nest of vipers; there's someone that is very poisonous that's feeding poison into the nation, but I am going to expose it if you pray for my glory." And the Lord says, "I am going to reveal myself, and Satan knows that there is a great revival, a great wind of God, the glorious God, that is coming to this nation and the Spirit of God is going to breathe upon this nation, so Satan wants to get in and stop what God is doing." But the Lord says to you, "I'm calling My army to arise, My army to stand up and lock shields, and if you will do this, you will see that I'm going to expose what's here and even in some rural communities . . .
>
> "Now you listen to me, the enemy likes to plant itself in these small little out of the way places, I'm going to expose, expose, expose, it's like a ring, it's like, different people in different places", but the Lord says: "I will not allow them to do the Mumbai type attack, where you do some simultaneous attacks", but the Lord says, "I am getting ready to pull the covers off, and if you pray, and if you stand", says the Lord, "I'm going to expose what is being done in secret. I will not only expose it, but it's going to shock the nation, like paddles to a heart, when someone is having a heart attack, and I'm going to use that to awaken the nation. For you are coming to a great awakening, a great awakening, for I'm going to wake up the nation", says the Lord, "and you're going to wake up either

through crisis or you're going to wake up through prayer . . .
"For I am calling My awakeners to arise", says the Lord, "that the glory of the Lord will be seen upon this nation! Arise, shine, for the light has come", says the Lord, "and the glory of the Lord will be revealed, for deep darkness is trying to cover the earth, but I am going to arise in the midst. So I say to My people, ARISE, ARISE, I'm calling for the prayer warriors and all the people to pray", says the Lord. And God says, "It can be averted totally . . . if you will stand and pray!"[11]

I dare say prophecies are more abundant at the beginning of the year than any other time, NEW YEAR offering an opportunity for a fresh start. I record three prophecies given in January of this year, 2015.

Firstly, PETER FINCH, a pastor in Ballyfermot, Dublin, received 3 words from the Lord which he has taught and expounded on at various events, including an apostolic leaders' event and a pastors' prayer day:

OUTBREAK   BREAK OUT   BREAKTHROUGH

At least two other people received the same Words from the LORD for Ireland in 2015, one being a young African woman who joined a group Peter had spoken at earlier in the day and gave the exact same words. Peter explains that *'Outbreak'* is the outbreak of the Holy Spirit. He describes this outbreak as "contagious, infectious, and uncontainable". In the natural, we see outbreaks of flesh-eating diseases, such as Ebola. So too, in the spiritual realm, things of the flesh–pride, prejudice, uncleanness and unforgiveness–will be eaten up. There will also be a loss of appetite for the things of the world. Secondly, *'Break out'* is release from control and confinement, breaking free from fear and intimidation and religious mindsets. Finally, *'Breakthrough'* has to do with possessing the promises of God and possessing new territory, defeating the spiritual enemy in our lives and land (2 Sam.5.17-25).

Embracing the plans God had for the New Year, I too received a word for the Christian body. The Lord said 2015 is a year of rest. Many would be called to a Sabbatical rest in this year. Of varying lengths, some would rest for days, weeks or months, others a whole year. People would begin their period of rest at different times. The one thing that would be the same is the purpose behind it–to come alone with God and hear His voice and heart's desire. Listening to Jesus, instead of busying ourselves in doing what we think He would want us to do, would enable us to do things far beyond our human capabilities. Indeed, this book is birthed out of such a time, the Lord asking me to spend 21 days with Him at the beginning of the year, before I would take up the challenge to compile and take it on tour in June 2015.

The third and final prophecy I share for 2015 is from BRENDA VANWINKLE, founder of Bespoken International, who, along with husband, Jim, feels privileged to have ministered in Ireland, both north and south, over the past few years. In January 2015 she wrote encouragingly:

> There is a gentleness in the breezes of the Spirit in Ireland that is capturable by a tender heart. There is a deep cry for justice that, like the fury of a storm off the sea, impacts all it touches as it resounds on its way from earth to heaven. Now, in a way that has not yet been seen on the earth – at least, not in our memories or lifetimes, or recorded in our written history books – the response to this cry is coming back from heaven to earth. What is coming is the sound of Flourishing.
>
> I see the island as a large green target, drawing to itself the Presence, the passion, the expression on earth of Emmanuel, God who is with us. It's as though with each day, each week, month and year that passes, the cadence of this distinctly Irish sound draws the Kingdom of God a step closer to itself by the very essence of how He fashioned it with His hand from the beginning. He delights in gardens! And has set aside for Himself a garden in the midst of the sea. A place of abundance. Hope. Courage. Joy. Creativity. Sound. Passion. Words. Movement. Laughter. Faithfulness. Sacrificial love. A very flourishing land, indeed. (These are not the idealistic dreams of an American who sees Ireland through a rose-colored lens. These are the thoughts, the impressions, the beliefs won through intercession and listening to the Father's heart. It is casting a vision of what can be, for those who have ears to hear.)
>
> The word flourish is worth being embraced! Filled with hopeful expectation for good, some of its meanings include: to grow luxuriantly; thrive; to reach a height of development or influence; to achieve success and prosper.
>
> While the season of flourishing has already begun, 2015 will mark an increase in the flourishing of Ireland. A battle is being waged for the identity and very soul of the island. Loud and well publicized voices would declare a name to take you back to what was. This name of yesteryear also begins with an 'f' – famine. However, what is past is past. It is over and gone. It is not and never again will be your identity – unless you choose it.

In this day, in this year, the Lord is holding out to you a new identity card, Ireland. On it is written, in bold and decorative letters, what He sees for your future. That word, that identity that will mark you from this day on, is FLOURISHING.

As the Kingdom of God is established on the earth in greater measure in the days to come, be ready for the sudden burst of thriving as a people, as nations. There is success and prosperity that will be available to you that, if received as sons and daughters, will enable you to become a storehouse for the nations of the earth. The earth needs you, Ireland. We need you to take your place. We need you to flourish.

A new sound is about to be released that will eclipse all other sounds for which you have been known in the past. The sound of flourishing in a land of justice and peace, joyful sobriety of heart and spirit, the unquenchable imagination of the redeemed. Music, invention, the movement of dance. Wisdom to steward and identity to carry the weight of that which previously was too much to dream of or hope for.

The land to which this new day is coming is, of course, not just the physical earth but the people who are of the land. I see it as a hand reaching down and connecting the power of heaven to a transformer that has been dark and waiting for its day to radiate across not just the island, but the nations of the earth. As you come alive in knowing who you truly are, the sparks will ignite a passion and fire for Truth in your Diaspora scattered in every nation around the globe.

Dear, humble, beautiful, treasured and desirable, Ireland, you have a destiny ahead of you that will shock not only yourself but the watching world. Many eyes are already on you; many more will be drawn to the life and solutions you carry as you walk in that for which you were created. Clothed with grace, filled with courage, displaying the goodness of the Father to an orphaned planet.

I bless you to FLOURISH.[12]

Lastly, we return to St. Patrick. Although 'St. Patrick's Breastplate' was written many centuries after his death, it is attributed to him. I include extracts from it, as something organically Irish, yet in this instance, written in different languages to represent, once again, the many cultures living side-by-side in Ireland. We begin the prayer in English and Irish, and then 'Christ with me' is shared between six languages.

St. Patrick's Breastplate (extracts)

I arise today
through a mighty strength, the invocation of the Trinity,
through belief in the Threeness,
through confession of the Oneness
of the Creator of creation.

I arise today
through the strength of Christ's birth with His baptism,
through the strength of His crucifixion with His burial,
through the strength of His resurrection with His ascension,
through the strength of His descent for the judgment of doom.

I arise today
through the strength of the love of cherubim,
In the obedience of angels,
In the service of archangels,
In the hope of resurrection to meet with reward,
In the prayers of patriarchs,
In the predictions of prophets,
In the preaching of apostles,
In the faith of confessors,
In the innocence of holy virgins,
In the deeds of righteous men . . .

I arise today, through
God's strength to pilot me,
God's might to uphold me,
God's wisdom to guide me,
God's eye to look before me,
God's ear to hear me,
God's word to speak for me,
God's hand to guard me,
God's shield to protect me,
God's host to save me
From snares of devils,
From temptation of vices,
From everyone who shall wish me ill,
afar and near . . .

Christ to shield me today
Against poison, against burning,
Against drowning, against wounding,
So that there may come to me an abundance of reward.

Lúireach Phádraig (in Irish)
(Aistrithe ag Pascal MacCofaigh)

Éirím inniu
Trí impí ar neart tréan na Trionóide,
Is creideamh ins an Triúr,
Trí dhearbhú aontacht
Chruthaitheora na n-uile ndúl.

Éirím inniu
Trí neart breithe Chríost is a bhaisteadh
Trí neart a chéasadh agus a adhlacadh,
Trí neart a aiséirí agus a dheasghabhála,
Trí neart a thuirlingthe Lá an Bhreithiúnais.

Éirím inniu trí neart grá na gCeiribím,
In umhlacht do na h-aingil,
I bhfreastal ar na hArdaingil,
Ag súil le toradh luachmhar an aiséirí,
In urnaithe na nArdathar,
I dtairngreachtaí na bhfáidh,
igcraobhscaoileadh na n-aspal,
igcreideamh coinfeasóirí,
ibhfíre maighdean naofa,
Ingníomhartha na bhfíréan . . .

Éirím inniu
Trí neart Dé dom stiúradh,
Cumhacht Dé do chumhdach,
Eagna Dé dom threorú,
Súil Dé ag breathnú romham,
Cluas Dé ag éisteacht liom,
Briathra Dé ag labhairt ar mo shon,
Lámh Dé dom chosaint,
Bealach Dé romham amach,
Sciath Dé dom chosaint,
Slua Dé dom thabhairt slán
Ó dhol na ndeamhan,
Ó mhealladh an pheaca,
Ó gach duine le droch-mhéin dom
Igcian is igcóngar . . .

Críost dom chumhdach inniu
Igcoinne nimhe, igcoinne loiscnigh,
Igcoinne bá, igcoinne gonta,
Idtreo go mbeidh toradh luachmhar, rafar ar mo shaothar

Christ with me...

Christ with me, *In Romanian:* Cristos cu mine,
Christ before me, Cristos înaintea mea,
Christ behind me, Cristos în urma mea,
Christ in me, Cristos în mine,

Translated by Maria and Romi Huian *from* Romania, *residing in Co. Cavan*

Christ beneath me, *In Swahili:* Kristo chini yangu,
Christ above me, Kristo juu yangu,
Christ on my right, Kristo kulia kwangu,
Christ on my left, Kristo kushoto kwangu,

Translated by Janet Craven, *retired missionary,* East Africa, *residing in Dublin*

Christ when I lie down, *In Spanish:* Cristo cuando me acuesto,
Christ when I sit down, Cristo cuando me siento,
Christ when I arise, Cristo cuando me levanto,

Translated by Martha Barrios De Finch *from* Venezuela, *pastor's wife in Dublin*

Christ in the heart of every man who thinks of me,
Christ in the mouth of everyone who speaks of me,
Christ in every eye that sees me,
Christ in every ear that hears me.

In Mandarin:

基督在每个想起我的人的心里
基督在每个讲到我的人的口中
基督在每个看见我的眼睛
基督在每个听到我的耳朵。

Translated by Kah Hoong Chang *from* Malaysia, *who met Jesus in Ireland.*

I arise today
Through a mighty strength, the invocation of the Trinity,
Through belief in the Threeness,
Through confession of the Oneness
of the Creator of creation.

In Irish: Érím inniu
Trí impí ar neart tréan na Trionóide,
Is creideamh ins an Triúr,
Trí dhearbhú aontacht
Chruthaitheora na n-uile ndúl.

Translated by Irishman, Pascal MacCofaigh, *Cork*

JOHN NEWTON, 1779

AMAZING GRACE

Amazing Grace - how sweet the sound!
That saved a wretch like me:
I once was lost, but now am found,
Was blind but now I see.

'Twas Grace that taught my heart to fear.
And Grace my fears relieved:
How precious did that grace appear
The hour I first believed!

Through many troubles, toils and snares
I have already come:
'Twas grace that brought me safe thus far
And grace shall lead me home.

The Lord has promised good to me;
His Word my hope secures:
He shall my Shield and Portion be
As long as life endures.

Yea, when my flesh and heart shall fail
And mortal life shall cease;
I shall posses within the veil
A life of joy and peace.

When we've been there ten thousand years,
Bright shining as the sun,
We've no less days to sing God's praise
Than when we first begun.

(English words for Irish translation, page 234)

But may the God of all grace, who called us to His eternal glory by Christ Jesus, after you have suffered a while, perfect, establish, strengthen, and settle you. To Him be the glory and the dominion forever and ever. Amen.

1 Peter 5: 10 NKJV

Endnotes

All prophetic words are used with permission. All published works are acknowledged below. The Editor does not necessarily agree with every view expressed by authors or with every interpretation of scripture made.

1. Extraordinary Religious Excitement in Ahoghill, Ballymena Observer, 26th March, 1859

2. Information provided by Paddy Monaghan, Adventures in Reconciliation

3. Information provided by Fr. Pat Collins http://patcollinscm.webs.com

4. This article is used with permission from Dominique Francois Email: all4ireland@gmail.com and was published on Elijah's List www.elijahlist.com

5. 'Is Prophecy about Catastrophe or Hope?' in 'He Has Anointed Me', Pat Collins CM (Luton: New Life, 2005), pp. 101-2

6. This article is used with permission from Catherine Brown, Founder/Director, Gatekeepers Global Ministries Co-Founder, Scottish Apostolic Networking Enterprise (www.gatekeepers.org.uk) and was published on Elijah's List www.elijahlist.com

7. Used with permission, transcribed by Linda Chrystal lchrystal@myfastmail.com

8. Used with permission from Sarah O'Neill http://johnandsarahoneill.blogspot.ie

9. Used with permission from Festus & Amy Alohan festusamy@mailcan.com

10. This article is used with permission from Sharon Stone, Christian International Europe www.cieurope.org published on Richard's Watch http://richards-watch.org

11. This article is used with permission from Cindy Jacobs and was published on Elijah's List www.elijahlist.com (Cindy Jacobs Generals International Email: generals@generals.org Website: generals.org)

13. This article is used with permission from Brenda Vanwinkle bespokeninternational.com

Bibliography

The Miracle of Ireland Edited by Daniel-Rops
1960 © Clenmore & Reynolds Ltd

Ireland's Lost Heritage © David Carnduff, 2003
ISBN: 0-9545647-0-7

Adventures in Reconciliation
1998 © Eugene Boyle and Paddy Monaghan, editors Eagle, Surrey GU2 5HN
ISBN: 0 86347 215 X

He Has Anointed Me © Pat Collins CM
Luton: New Life, 2005